UNAPOLOGETICALLY
SUPERNATURAL

UNAPOLOGETICALLY
SUPERNATURAL

REAL-WORLD EMPOWERMENT

FOR OUT OF THIS WORLD

MIRACLES

DARREN STOTT

DESTINY IMAGE® PUBLISHERS, INC.

P.O. Box 310, Shippensburg, PA 17257-0310

"Publishing cutting-edge prophetic resources to supernaturally empower the body of Christ"

This book and all other Destiny Image and Destiny Image Fiction books are available at Christian bookstores and distributors worldwide.

For more information on foreign distributors, call 717-532-3040.

Reach us on the Internet: www.destinyimage.com.

ISBN 13 TP: 978-0-7684-7448-0

ISBN 13 eBook: 978-0-7684-7449-7

ISBN 13 Hardcover: 978-0-7684-8116-7

ISBN 13 Large Print: 978-0-7684-81150

For Worldwide Distribution.

1 2 3 4 5 6 7 8 / 28 27 26 25 24

DEDICATION

To our four amazing children:

As I write these words, I am filled with a sense of pride and gratitude for the gifts you are to your mom and me. Abigail Rose, Peter Joseph, Sophia Zoe, and Victoria Stott. You are our greatest joy!

I dedicate this book, *Unapologetically Supernatural*, to each of you. You are the fourth generation of supernaturalists in our family. I am so proud of how you embrace and celebrate the supernatural reality of the kingdom of heaven without reservation.

As you journey through life, remember that you are unique and valuable. You were created for a purpose, and you have the potential to do great things for the glory of God. Don't be afraid to be yourself and stay true to your beliefs, even when the world or the church tries to put you in a box.

Mom and I will always be here to support you, love you, and cheer you on as you pursue Christ and the desires He has put in your heart. Remember, you are not alone, for God is always with you.

May the pages of *Unapologetically Supernatural* inspire and encourage you on this wild adventure called life.

This is my dedication to you, my dear world changers.

With love,

Dad

CONTENTS

INTRODUCTION

"The supernatural is not an option for the Christian; it is a necessity."

—WATCHMAN NEE

WHY YOU SHOULD READ THE INTRODUCTION

The young couple barged into my office, creating a whirlwind of tension that made the room feel like it was about to implode. The air was thick with anger and frustration, and it was clear that something had gone awry. The young man, usually full of life, was now sulking like a dog that had just been scolded for chewing up a slipper. His fiancée, on the other hand, was still fuming and itching to get something off her chest.

As I closed my eyes to begin the prayer, she couldn't hold back any longer. "Well, are you going to tell Pastor Darren, or will you make me do it?" she exclaimed, her voice sharp as a razor. The young man muttered a response, his head still

hanging low as he avoided my gaze. "Yes, I will tell him, but I don't think it's a big deal," he mumbled.

His fiancée was having none of it. "It is a big deal to me! I take our relationship seriously, and I wish you did too," she shot back.

"I'm taking it seriously!" he protested weakly.

"Then just tell him!" she snapped.

Finally, he looked up at me and explained his transgression. "She's mad at me because I didn't read the book's introduction. I told her that nobody reads the introduction of a book, that if you read the book, reading the introduction is just a waste of time."

I raised an eyebrow, trying my best not to laugh. "Well, did you at least read the rest of the book?"

"Yes, I did! And I loved it and can't wait to discuss it," he answered eagerly.

His fiancée rolled her eyes and shook her head in exasperation. "You foolish fool. Don't you know, without a well-crafted introduction, a book risks losing its reader's attention and failing to establish the necessary tone and context for the rest of the text, highlighting the critical role that introductions play in engaging and informing readers!"

I couldn't help but chuckle at her passionate defense of the importance of introductions. "Well, it seems like we're all on the same page now," I said with a smile. "Let's just take a deep breath and get started."

As we began our discussion, I couldn't help but think about how silly the situation was. But then again, maybe it was a good reminder that the little things can sometimes cause the most significant problems.

Listen up, my friend. If you're serious—and I mean truly serious—about unlocking the fullness of your supernatural identity and destiny, then whatever you do, don't skip this introduction.

THE GOOD NEWS AND THE BAD NEWS

The supernatural has become a popular topic in recent times, even among those who were once hesitant to embrace it. From the most conservative to the most open-minded, there is an increasing interest in the things of the Holy Spirit. Even the Baptists are singing Bethel songs these days. However, while this new openness presents a unique opportunity for believers to engage in supernatural experiences, it also brings a growing concern for the influx of non-biblical and nonsensical practices emerging among followers of Jesus Christ.

How do we encourage, equip, and empower believers to embrace the supernatural without losing sight of the gospel mission and biblical inerrancy as we navigate this landscape?

How can we become 100 percent unapologetically supernatural without becoming a bunch of weird, woo-woo hippies?

1. Know who you already are in Christ.

A dog can't try to be a dog because a dog is already a dog. But if a dog doesn't know he's a dog, he may waste time, energy, and money trying to become something he already is. Similarly, in Christ you are already unapologetically supernatural. This book won't make you supernatural, but it will provide you with the language and blueprint to make sense of your identity.

2. Remember, Jesus is enough.

In the kingdom, there are no shortcuts or quick fixes. The supernatural is not meant to manipulate people or outcomes; that's the definition of witchcraft.

No crystal, oil, holy water, church membership, or spiritual excursion can replace the power and authority of Jesus. He is everything. He is the way, the truth, and the life. He is the only way to the Father. Don't be distracted by someone else's supernatural "keys" or methods; they are not Christ Himself. Our focus should always be on our Bridegroom, and through our love and devotion to Him, we can be confident that we will finish our race well.

3. Understand the role of supernatural experiences.

In the church, there can be misunderstandings about the purpose and significance of supernatural experiences. Some may see these experiences as a badge of honor, a mark of being part of an elite group of chosen people. This perspective can lead to a dangerous pride and sense of superiority, opening the door to a spirit of stupidity. Conversely, others may feel discouraged or even condemned if they have not had such experiences, seeing themselves as less spiritual or as having done something wrong. However, the truth is that while supernatural encounters can be powerful and transformative, they are not an end in themselves. They are simply a means to an end, a way to draw closer to God and fulfill His purposes for our lives.

In this book, we will help you understand the supernatural storyline of the Bible and your role within it. By providing a clear framework for understanding supernatural experiences, we will help you stay grounded and avoid becoming unfruitful or strange.

Our goal is to motivate you to act and provide a strong sense of purpose and accountability so that you can fully embrace your supernatural identity and walk in the fullness of all God has for you.

I'M NOT "THAT GUY"; I AM "THAT GUY!"

For clarification, let me state upfront that I am not a person who constantly preaches caution and restraint at every turn. I don't have a doctorate in Hebrew, and I'm not interested in engaging in public debates about theological minutiae. You won't find me on the airwaves, fervently arguing about scripture, nor will you catch me wearing the latest designer cologne (I rely on a modest application of non-scented Arm & Hammer baking soda deodorant).

I'm not a pessimist by nature, nor do I harbor any deep-seated anger or resentment. I'm not a fan of crass appeals to emotion, such as the use of pornography in altar calls, and I don't see the value in needlessly disparaging the church on social media.

I am a supernaturalist.

I've actually been running my own ministry called Supernaturalist Ministries since 2013. I've been hosting the Supernaturalist Podcast Show for over a decade. I've had the pleasure of interviewing some of our generation's most prominent supernatural leaders.

Here's a little tidbit for you: back in January of 2022, I received a text message from none other than Larry Sparks of Destiny Image Publishers. He told me, "Darren, how about you write a book called *The Supernaturalist*?"

I didn't waste any time before responding, "Let's go!"

But wouldn't you know it? Just a few months later, some other supernaturalist minister from my city published his book with that exact same title. Go figure.

Let me be clear; I am absolutely "that guy." I'm proud to run with the glory weirdos, to be counted among the wild and burning ones. I make no apologies for my unapologetically supernatural beliefs and practices.

But here's the thing: it's not just me. My family is cut from the same cloth. We've been steeped in the supernatural from day one. My dad was a man who regularly got drunk in the spirit and received his travel directions from angels who would draw maps in lightning on the walls of his hotel room.

As I write this, I'm currently deep in the heart of the Indian jungle. Today, my children and I ministered in a village where no white missionaries had ever set foot. My 12-year-old son and 14-year-old daughter preached fearlessly, sharing the visions they'd received from the Lord. And today was historic: pastors and Hindu government leaders came together to celebrate American missionaries in a state where foreigners preaching the gospel is entirely against the law.

So yes, I'm "that guy." But I wouldn't have it any other way.

Regarding the Holy Spirit, I have a reputation for getting after it!

Let me be clear: I may be "that guy" who runs with the glory weirdos and embraces the supernatural with unbridled passion, but that doesn't mean I'm random, foolish, or goofy.

Quite the opposite is true. I have a purpose: to share the good news of the supernatural Gospel of Jesus Christ with the world. I am a strategic thinker, my degree is in Bible & Theology, and I live to awaken people to their supernatural identity and destiny in Jesus Christ.

So yes, I'm unconventional. I'm radical. I'm a bit of a maverick. But I'm still serious, focused, and purposeful in all that I do. I believe in the power of the supernatural to transform lives, heal bodies, and change the world. And I'll stop at nothing to see that vision become a reality.

BUT DON'T WORRY!

But don't worry—this book is the solution! It's a supernatural manifesto guiding you toward real-world empowerment and out-of-this-world miracles. It's practical, divinely inspired, and will cover everything from miracles and dreams to paranormal creatures like Bigfoot, astral projection, and lucid dreaming. The only things we won't discuss are dieting, budgeting, and sex—those topics will have to wait for future books.

If you practice what you learn in this book, you will awaken to who you are as a supernatural being and begin to function in a next-level supernatural authority. You will have dreams and encounters, walk in miracles, gain wisdom and revelation, and if you are in a cult, you will be given the tools and keys to finding a biblical supernatural community called a church.

So get ready to dive into the supernatural with confidence, knowledge, and authority. This book will change everything.

How will we do this?

Let me give you a glimpse of what you can expect from this book.

First, we will awaken you to your supernatural identity. It will take some teaching, convincing, and stripping away of defeatist beliefs that aim to hold you back from everything Jesus has in store for you.

Then we will explore why most people don't experience the supernatural power of King Jesus regularly. We will reveal the secret ingredient that allows you to see supernatural demonstrations and empowers you to walk in the supernatural consistently.

In Chapter Three, we will help you set your supernatural trajectory practically. Many people stumble around in the supernatural, needing to consistently learn how to grow in signs, wonders, and miracles. We will give you the key to supernatural growth and acceleration at an unprecedented rate.

Chapter Four will dive into what you need to know to sniff out counterfeit prophetic movements and false prophets. If you embrace your supernatural identity, establishing guard rails is essential. This will benefit you and help others who are being lured in by unhealthy, manipulative, and, in some cases, evil counterfeit shepherds and communities.

Chapter Five will focus on the need for a good and healthy supernatural community. We will provide you with a biblical road map for a supernatural church's composition, requirements, and benefits.

In Chapter Six, we will teach you how to activate the realm of miracles in your life. Get ready to step into greater boldness and practical steps to see impossibilities bow before the feet of Jesus.

In Chapter Seven, we will guide you on establishing your authority regarding night factors such as sleep, rest, and dreams. You will love this chapter as we delve into some wild stuff.

In Chapter Eight, we talk about the supernatural battle taking place on earth, including demonic portals opening and paranormal creatures. If you are going to be unapologetically supernatural, you must not be ignorant of the war taking place in our culture in plain sight.

In Chapter Nine, we talk about the only way to displace this present darkness, and here's a clue: through a company of priests. You will discover that God is raising up a priesthood in this hour to operate as the literal body and authority of Jesus on earth, giving Him a voice and presence here.

This book is your supernatural manifesto, your guide to real-world empowerment for out-of-this-world miracles.

Get ready to be awakened to who you really are and to function in next-level supernatural authority.

CHAPTER ONE

HOW TO UNLOCK THE SUPERNATURAL REALMS OF HEAVEN

"Part of the problem with the word disabilities is that it immediately suggests an inability to see or hear or walk or do other things that many of us take for granted. But what of people who can't feel? Or talk about their feelings? Or manage their feelings in ways? What of people who aren't able to form close and strong relationships? And people who cannot find fulfillment i n their lives, or those who have lost hope, who live in disappointment and bitterness and find in life no joy, no love? These, it seems to me, are the real disabilities."

–FRED ROGERS, *The World According to Mister Rogers*[1]

You Are Supernatural!

You, my friend, are supernatural! Yes, you heard it right! You may not have fully realized it, but an awe-inspiring supernatural God created you for an extraordinary and supernatural purpose!

Once we dive deep into the supernatural storyline of the Bible and understand our unique role in it, you'll have the courage to shout out loud, "I am unapologetically supernatural!"

Let's try it now! Take a deep breath and yell, "I am unapologetically supernatural!"

How did it feel? Did it feel true? Did you actually do it?

The main reason why there may be cognitive dissonance around claiming to be supernatural is that you may not feel very supernatural, and yet, feelings aside, the number-one reason why most people wouldn't consider themselves to be supernatural is that they have already disqualified their present selves because of the nature of the subconscious comparison.

Comparison is the number-one reason why we disqualify the present us from the supernatural category.

Comparison Has a Voice

This isn't the first supernatural book that you have read, right? You enjoy reading about the encounters, realms, and miracles that others have walked in. When we hear about those who are further ahead of us in any area of life, we subconsciously compare ourselves to them. The problem is that comparison has a voice, and he works through obnoxious questioning.

Questions like, "Are you where these amazing people are? If not, could you be? When could you be? And what's keeping you from being there?" In the garden, the serpent tempted Adam and Eve with obnoxious questioning to get them to compare themselves to Yahweh.

After underscoring the comparison, he offered them the choice to disobey as the gateway to promotion, ascension, and equal divine intelligence with Yahweh.

When overwhelmed by obnoxious questioning, most people avoid the pain associated with analyzing the comparisons and put the person into a "hero category." Or if a spirit of jealousy is ruling you, you will find a reason to disqualify them, putting them into the "villain category."

HEROES OF THE FAITH

There's nothing wrong with having heroes of the faith. I have many heroes! Two of my favorite heroes are William Branham and Bobby Conner.

William Branham

On April 6, 1909, William Branham was born. As his 15-year-old mom held him in her arms, his grandma opened the blinds, and as she did, a beautiful supernatural orb of light shot through the window. It wasn't a spiritual ball of light that you had to have spiritual eyes to see. And everybody in the room saw a living physical ball of fire, probably about the size of a beach ball. William says it "whirled" into the room and then began "whirling" around him until it settled down and rested on his bed.

Bobby Conner

Modern-day contemporary prophet Bobby Conner shares about his father, who was put away because he lost his mind due to a venereal disease. The doctor told Bobby's mom that the baby in the womb would surely be born with the same disease, so she determined to self-abort the baby by inserting a coat hanger up and into her uterus. As the sharp coat hanger approached baby Bobby, the hand of God moved Bobby up and to the side so that the wire missed him.

As an adult, the Lord showed Bobby what had happened in the womb. When Bobby inquired of his mom about the accuracy of the vision, she confirmed that every word was as Bobby had witnessed. God supernaturally protected Bobby as he was to be a modern prophet to the church and the nations.

Darren Stott

When Darren Stott was born (that's me), no whirling light orb circled my mom and rested on my bed, and the hand of God never moved me aside in the womb. Compared to Billy and Bobby, my birth seems quite natural. If I didn't have a miraculous supernatural birth story, how could I be anything like William Branham or Bobby Conner?

JOHN G. LAKE'S MANTLE

I am going to use John G. Lake's mantle as a metaphor. I have the honor of leading an organization called the Renaissance Coalition. The organization was started by John G. Lake in South Africa in 1908 and incorporated in Spokane,

Washington, by his daughter and son-in-law in 1947, making it the oldest organization in the state of Washington.

When asked if we have John G. Lake's mantle, we respond with, "No." We don't claim to have Lake's mantle because not even John G. Lake had his mantle. Lake walked in the anointing of Christ and desired that a generation of Christ-people would walk in the fullness of power, not pulling authority from Lake's legacy but from the virtue of the Ancient of Days.

The world doesn't need another John G. Lake, William Branham, Bobby Conner, or Darren Stott. The earth needs you. You are filled with the Holy Spirit and walk with bold clarity and courage. Comparison is a spirit, and it's not of the Holy Spirit. It grows from a foundation of pride and insecurity, and God loves you too much to allow these ingredients to be part of your DNA.

Comparison may suggest that you are merely human, as your life may appear natural and ordinary. However, do not underestimate your prophetic storyline. Paul would say it like this, "You are Christ's workmanship" (see Ephesians 2:10). The power of the Holy Spirit lies within you. Throughout your life, moments of divine intervention and supernatural encounters have shaped your path and purpose. By reflecting back on these significant instances with intentionality, the Holy Spirit will reveal the significance of your life. Let me help you rediscover the compelling evidence for your supernatural backstory.

YOUR SUPERNATURAL PAST

He has made everything beautiful in its time. He has also set eternity in the human heart; yet no one can fathom what God has done from beginning to end (Ecclesiastes 3:11 NIV).

In her book *The Mind of the Maker*, Dorothy Sayers presents the trinity as consisting of the Creative Idea, the Creative Energy, and the Creative Power. The Creative Idea, the image of the Father, is not bound by time and exists outside of it. It is passionless and timeless and sees the whole work complete at once, with the end in the beginning.

As Ecclesiastes 3:11 states, *"God has made everything beautiful in its time."* This divine system of order and beauty was in place before creation began, including the development of humanity, with an eternal plan in place. Romans 8:28 further confirms that all things work together for good in this divine system.

It is mind-blowing to realize that God has embedded the record of eternity into every human being. As a result, each person begins to see their supernatural origin story over time.

LIBERATING YOUR MEMORIES

While reading this chapter, get your journal and pen and try out this exercise. Ask the Holy Spirit to supernaturally jog your memory. Thank Jesus for the ability to remember scenes and moments that you have since forgotten. By faith, write out a list of supernatural things you saw as a baby, a child, a teenager, and a young adult. You might remember seeing angels, demons, heaven, or hell.

I remember one such night as a child waking and looking out my bedroom window to see stairs connecting heaven with our front yard and angels casually walking up and down the stairs. It was like a heavenly highway.

Keep writing and writing until every moment that you can remember is on the pages. It might take a few days or even a few weeks. You will discover how your past is full of supernatural happenings, even more than you remembered. You probably are also recalling a lot of details that you had forgotten. Write down as much detail as you possibly can.

When comparing our lives to others, the comparison isn't fair, and the reason is that we are comparing someone else's list of supernatural encounters with where we are at, right there, at that moment. Once you catalog your supernatural occurrences, you will see that you are unapologetically supernatural.

It doesn't just pertain to you. The supernatural is a normal part of every person's childhood and upbringing, and this is because the spiritual realm is a dimension that God created for us. When we are born, there are no filters or preconceived veils. In fact, there is a supernatural intensity that is too much for many children to process through, and this is where many parents disable the spiritual sensitivity of their children by programming their kids with declarations that dishonor their spiritual sight, such as, "What you are experiencing is not real; it is just your imagination."

One night my daughter Abigail was crying, so I went into her bedroom to see what was wrong. She pointed toward the closet and said something was in the closet. When I looked in the closet, I saw a demon move quickly in front of me. In my head, I thought, *What the heck! There really is something in her closet!* I rebuked it out loud in the name of Jesus, and it disappeared. I told Abigail not to worry and informed her that we had taken care of it. She knew I was telling the truth because she could see it was gone. She was no longer afraid. She rolled over and went back to sleep. However, my heart was still pounding.

FINDING JESUS IN YOUR PAST

Have you ever seen Jesus? Most people might think they haven't; however, most people have. The question isn't have we seen Jesus, but did we recognize Him when we saw Him?

Let's do the same thing we did before and ask the Holy Spirit to reveal any moments in your past when you saw Jesus when He came to you. In a dream, in a vision, or while awake. Ask the Holy Spirit to show you moments you've forgotten or that He revealed Himself to you, but you didn't know it was Him.

As you are beginning to remember these supernatural occurrences from your past and maybe even moments when Jesus revealed Himself to you, you will notice that something remarkable is taking place. These moments, perhaps forgotten, are becoming colorful and vivid in a more real way. It is how the kingdom of heaven works. Honor unlocks the fullness of our testimony, and our testimony creates the ability to remember more and lock it in through belief.

Because these supernatural occurrences are old and in our past, we don't look for them, and because we don't look for them, we don't find them, thereby accepting a subconscious lie that they are not there. But they are!

When we inform people that the record of the supernatural is within their timeline, then, with the power of the Holy Spirit and a posture of honor, we can begin to see this evidence of God's grace in our history.

Not only is this true for us, but it is valid for others. Similarly, I'm walking you through this process, and you can walk other people through this as well. When people begin to see how God has been pursuing them as far back as they can remember, people will begin to see how loved they are. Not only that, but they will get confidence that God wants to move in their lives, especially supernaturally.

HOW TO UNLOCK THE SUPERNATURAL REALMS OF HEAVEN

Having established that the supernatural has been embedded within your storyline, the record of eternity is in your timeline. Though powerful yet forgotten encounters with Jesus may also be there, we must go deeper.

Now, we address the question of what we must do to unlock the supernatural realms of heaven. The realms of the supernatural may have felt like the Wild West in your past. Perhaps you lacked the understanding, theology, and authority needed to navigate through what you were experiencing. Because of the confusion, brokenness, and maybe even darkness in that previous era of the supernatural, you left it behind you and were put in a room with a locked door.

If you look back, you will see that the lock was artificial. God never locked you out of heaven. You locked yourself out. William Blake resolved this issue when he wrote these words in *The*

Marriage of Heaven and Hell: "If the doors of perception were cleansed, everything would appear to man as it is: infinite."

The truth is the supernatural realms of heaven are open to you, and His heart is unlocked. The possibilities are endless. It's not God's heart that we must address; it is your heart. If you are willing to open up, you will find that heaven is already open to you. If you are willing for your spirit man to be received and loved, then you will find the Holy Spirit is already willing and prepared to catapult you into a supernatural life full of God's wonder.

Our worship songs and prayers often make it sound like we are knocking on heaven's door, but that isn't biblical, as affirmed in Revelation 3:20 (NASB), *"Behold, I stand at the door and knock."* It is Jesus knocking on our door! Many people see this classic picture of Jesus knocking on an old wooden door, and they equate it to a picture of salvation.

The verse of Jesus standing at the door knocking is based on a text that is not referring to unbelievers or salvation, but the context is Jesus pleading to the church of Laodicea. Believers have locked Jesus outside, where He is saying, "If anyone hears my voice and opens the door, I will come in and eat with that person, and they with me."

Right now, Jesus is standing outside your door and is looking for communion with you. We are not necessarily talking about your salvation but the opportunity to rediscover the joy of your salvation. If you are ready to see the realms of the supernatural unlocked in your life, you will have to begin by trusting Jesus again and unlocking your heart.

THE VILLAIN

Here's where it gets real, where I tell it to you straight. I might tell you some things that you probably already know. Still, you must hear it again anyway, and when I say it, even though you already know it, what I'm about to tell you will come as a relief because of the language for what you've been discerning. You are supernatural, and you have a supervillain!

He is known as the Serpent, Lucifer, Satan, Beelzebub, Diabolo, or Old Nick (an informal nickname for the devil from the 1600s, ironically close to Old Saint Nick).

Having walked with Jesus all that time, John and Peter were familiar with the devil as a thief and adversary. In John 10:10, it is mentioned that the thief comes only to steal and kill and destroy. The devil is mentioned as a thief 16 times in the New Testament. And 1 Peter 5:8 (NASB) says, "*Your adversary, the devil, prowls around like a roaring lion, seeking someone to devour.*"

The Greek word *antidikos* (from *anti* = against + *dike* = a cause or suit at law) was used first as a word for an opponent in a lawsuit and then came to mean an adversary or enemy without reference to legal affairs. It describes one who is actively and continuously hostile toward someone. An adversary contends with, opposes, or resists. *Diabolos* (devil) is the noun form of the verb *diaballō*, which describes those who bring a false charge against one, but also those who disseminate the truth concerning someone and do so maliciously, insidiously, and with hostility. *The Wuest Bible Study* describes it as "to riddle one with accusations."[2]

You now comprehend the malicious tactics employed by the enemy, utilizing thievery and false accusations. Like any nefarious villain, his sole purpose is to promote injustice. Can you fathom a life dedicated solely to rejecting love, joy, and peace offered by the Holy Spirit, and persistently fighting against it? This opposition to harmony represents the very core of injustice—the act of unraveling the intricate threads of supernatural, relational, and cultural unity that comprise shalom. Yet, while injustice seeks to unravel these threads, they can be rewoven and restored to their original purpose of peace.

A Picture of Today's Church

The villain hates all people, all image bearers of Yahweh, especially those who are knit together to function as the body of Christ, the ecclesia, which is the church. These are those who are deputized to reweave the fabric of shalom. The villain is determined to obstruct the identity and destiny of the ecclesia and has remained steadfast in his number-one strategy since the beginning. This strategy involves exploiting natural hardships to manipulate and create emotional turmoil, allowing him to spread lies. The ultimate goal is to gradually construct a false identity of Yahweh using disappointment as a foundation. The tragedies will serve as the passion needed to disguise deferred hope as good theology.

Imagine having a dad who was rich and powerful, and yet he wasn't able to provide for your basic needs. And because he was *so* rich and powerful, he was forced to use his time and attention to govern his responsibilities, forcing him to neglect you. You, however, did not resent your father for his neglect because, after all, he was so powerful that subconsciously you began to believe that to survive, you would have to figure out how to take care of yourself, completely independent from a relationship or any actual trust in your father. Now imagine that you were convinced that your pride in your independence was how you would please and honor him.

It is a picture of many in the modern church. We believe in God. We love God. We serve God. We know He could do and has done extraordinary things. We know that He is capable of stepping into our modern-day messes, yet He probably won't. He's far too powerful to interfere with our meager human turmoil.

So we work on maturing our ability to manage life's affairs on our own while maintaining an integral set of principles and moral ideals independent of intimacy with our Father God while declaring absolute and total dependence on Him. Now we wonder why the gospel doesn't seem appealing to those who do not yet subscribe to our faith.

If gospel means good news, and it does, how can *this* be the gospel? It is not good news at all. How could we demand that people swear total dependence on Yahweh, yet this God shows little to no reciprocation? How can we demand that people draw nearer to God without presenting a true picture of a loving Father who longs to draw near to them?

For too long, unsupervised orphan theology void of any supernatural presence has painted a picture of an absent God who is too busy for His children and yet religiously demands total trust and submission. This is the fruit of hope deferred within the church. The villain has exploited natural hardships for hundreds of years while embedding lies into the church's culture.

It is problematic because countless children don't know who their daddy is, which is why we don't see more signs, wonders, and miracles. Somebody needs to do something! And that somebody is you. An unapologetically supernatural generation is about to execute kingdom justice on earth.

Hope deferred is what locks the gates of the supernatural realms of glory and is what keeps us always wanting to elevate other people into categories of supernatural heroism while never leaning into the injustice for ourselves and making things right. Hope deferred is simply the fruit of the villain's lies, costing your life of abundance and the revelation of your call and destiny.

UNLOCK THE GATES

So there, I said it; you've been lied to. The world has lied to you. Religion has lied to you, and the chief of lies has lied to you. We wouldn't expect any less out of the liar. And now the truth is you have a heavenly Father who loves you, created you in His image and likeness, and assigned you to the earth for such a time as this. You're fearfully and wonderfully made, and the earth needs you.

Hell has thrown everything against you, and yet you are still standing. Having done all, you have stood firm. You have stood against the wiles of the enemy. You have fallen, but you've gotten back up. You've been beaten up by the bad and good guys, and you have often wondered if there are any good guys. And even though you have questioned everything, you know I'm right when I tell you that in light of everything that you have faced, His grace has been sufficient because it is sufficient. You are still standing because of God's grace, for none of us can boast in our own strength.

It's time to unlock the gates and let the glory of the Lord begin to come up and out of you. It is not something that heaven has to unlock on its side; this is a lock that must be addressed from our side. With God's faithfulness, we must confront the pain of the past. We have to tell our souls that the pain was not punishment; our punishment fell on Jesus, all of it.

The pain was not proof of God's passivity or lack of love toward us. He was there in the past, just as He is in the present, with His arms and heart wide open, longing to reveal His fatherly nature and faithful presence within our trial.

The key to unlocking the supernatural realms of heaven is not what you might think, for if these gates were locked by hope deferred, then one might assume that hope would be the key that unlocks them, but this is not so. The key that unlocks these supernatural portals of glory is trust. The question I must ask you, though I do not want to, is this:

"Are you willing to trust the Lord with your past, present, and future?"

If your answer is yes, then you are ready to move forward, but if your answer is no, then we have to go backward to deal with the hurts of the past, to find Jesus in the trials so that we can extract the lies and release the truth into those wounds to administrate proper healing.

Trust is a big deal. Trust is the foundation of any relationship. If you don't have trust, you will lack the grit to go through intense conflict and confrontation. But if you have trust, you'll be able to walk through any flame, and it will not destroy you; it will only make you stronger.

> *Trust in the Lord with all your heart,*
>
> *and do not lean on your own understanding.*
>
> *In all your ways acknowledge him,*
>
> *and he will make straight your paths* (Proverbs 3:5-6 ESV).

DISMANTLING TRUST DEFEATERS

If we're going to unlock the supernatural realms of heaven, we must address defeater beliefs. Defeater beliefs are any beliefs we believe to be true that are rooted in a lie and keep us from God's best for our lives. Here are five examples of defeater beliefs, and I suggest that perhaps you might be able to find additional beliefs that have been hiding in your subconscious and influencing you without you even realizing it.

These five examples are only examples; they are to help you understand how defeater beliefs work so that you can identify them. I want you to partner with the Holy Spirit to continue to discern lies—beliefs that include the words *always*, *never*, or any expectations you are assuming are inevitable despite your desire or the Lord's. You will see that these defeaters are basic assumptions, and assumptions are simply judgments. Judgments conducted outside of truth are powerful in the spirit realm, allowing deception to set one's destiny coordinates.

The Five Examples

1. "God cannot be trusted."

I believed this lie but didn't know I believed it. I would never have said it out loud. When God called me into the ministry, I told the Lord that if I said yes and obeyed Him, He had better not treat me like He treated my parents. It was at this point He responded by telling me that I was believing this lie and that I didn't trust Him. I admitted He was right, and then I broke down crying.

Little did I know that my lack of trust resulted in me being my functional savior. If I couldn't trust God, then how could I trust people? So I lived for myself and did what made me happy because, in doing so, there would be someone looking out for me. But my deception was only hurting me.

In my attempt to preserve and protect my joy, I kept myself from experiencing it. The lie that *God could not be trusted* framed a faulty theological structure. My bad beliefs influenced bad behaviors, and the Lord told me He was unwilling to partner with me unless I was willing to trust Him completely. A partnership will work no other way.

I was starting to see the absolute absurdity of it, but I thought, *If I can't trust God, I am saying that I'm going to put all my trust in myself.* I might not have been the smartest dude, but I wasn't that big of an idiot. With tears spraying out of my eyes, I finally broke and muttered aloud, "God, I trust You," and it's the best thing I've ever done.

2. "People will always let me down."

After being a pastor for some time now, I have found this particular lie to be one of the most common subconscious defeater beliefs that keep people from being able to trust. They will come to our church, hoping that maybe our church will be different and believing for a while that our church is the best thing since sliced cheese.

However, over time, they begin to pull back, not because anything negative has happened, but because there is this expectation that it is just a matter of time until history repeats itself. So they sabotage the possibility of intimate connection, vulnerability, and true partnership. Many people are done with their past. But unfortunately, the past isn't done with them.

3. "If I trust a church again, it's just a matter of time until they hurt and reject me."

Community is one of the most misunderstood and under-rated forces on the earth. The Tower of Babel in Genesis 11 demonstrates the potential of a unified community. God had to step down and bring disunity to the community because the hazards would have been lethal for humanity. We get messed up in family settings, but we can ultimately get restored in family settings.

For this reason, there is more warfare around the church and family than any other dynamic on the earth. If the enemy can keep families disunified and broken, if he can keep the church divided and disillusioned, then he can have unfettered access and unlimited influence without accountability or consequence. Church hurt is real. Pastors attack people. People attack pastors. Leadership and denominations take sides. Everybody writes their names on statements and creeds. Votes. Splits. Numerous combinations of possible deconstructions and numerous resulting curses and consequences. I am the chief of church hurt victims. I went from being a young prince in the kingdom of my father's church to believing the lie that I was an orphan, disillusioned and bitter while vowing to have nothing to do with the institution.

However, it wasn't until God dealt with my unforgiveness and planted a desire in my heart to return to the church that I could engage with my true identity and destiny. What I am saying is this: if I had not returned to the church, and in my case, the place where my heart was broken (typically not something I would recommend), then I would not have been able to receive the destiny scroll for my life.

Destiny dies in self-preservation, and self-protection may be essential for a season but it's no way to live your life. I can assure you of this—every person will have their heart hurt, and yes, it hurts, but a wounded heart is no reason to live a fruitless existence. There is nothing more courageous than one who loved and lost and yet chose to love again—than one who chose to trust again after their trust had been crushed. This tremendous feat requires faith and the grace of Jesus Christ. No matter what you have faced, His grace is sufficient.

4. "I cannot be trusted. I am bad news."

Perhaps your problem isn't that you don't trust God or don't trust people. Perhaps the thought of being in a community with God and man is exhilarating to you. Maybe your problem is that you don't trust yourself. Maybe you have even word-cursed yourself by telling others that you cannot be trusted because *you will always screw things up.* Or maybe you don't want to join a church because you're afraid you will somehow curse the church or sabotage its momentum.

I once had a man tell me that every church he attends ends up getting destroyed. I gave him a big hug and said, "Welcome! You are not powerful enough to destroy this church. It belongs to Jesus." He sighed a deep breath of relief.

Perhaps you see yourself as bad news, not even wanting to date because you believe you will ruin the other person's life. Now, perhaps the reality is that you've messed up a lot of things, you have been the cause of countless divorces, and you have even been the source of a church split or two. What is needed here is not mere encouragement or some daily prophetic declarations. What you will need are a Savior and a complete and total swapperoo. The truth is that you do not have to be cursed or be a curse when you understand Deuteronomy 21:23, *"Cursed is he who hangs on a tree."*

Jesus became your curse! On the cross, He became your corruption, your sin, your shame, and your sequence of self-instigated and unfortunate circumstances. When He hung from the tree, He didn't die *for* you; He died *as* you. His resurrection from death and defeat invites you to participate in this huge and glorious achievement. Jesus not only endured the most extreme of hardships, but He also overcame them, He conquered them, and His victory created a portal by which you are invited to cross the threshold.

For you to take on His good name, you will have to be willing for Him to take on your bad name. For you to take on the record of righteousness, you must be willing to trust Him with your record of unrighteousness. Your depraved nature and its extremity must be buried with Him in that tomb. It is essential to let go of the pride associated with your corruption and embrace the humility that comes with receiving His unmerited forgiveness. Your new nature in Christ makes you trustworthy and righteous—100 percent blameless! You do not have to metaphorically chain yourself to a tree like a village monster. Stop glorifying the bigness of your badness; let it die and the memories it conjures up. Stop talking about the pain you've caused and start living a new life of intimacy with Christ. With Jesus as your Savior, you can be truly and immediately liberated from your fear of yourself. I can assure you that Jesus is not afraid of you. Not at all.

5. "I will always be alone."

Isolation in and of itself is one of the greatest illusions, and when we understand the dynamics of the spirit world, we know we are never alone. It can be both good or bad, depending on the realm that you are living in. When we believe we are isolated, that lie enables us to live outside any intimacy or accountability that would produce fruitfulness. If anybody could have survived in isolation and possibly even thrived, it would have been Jesus. And yet the first thing He did, even before starting His ministry, was recruit His disciples. None of us can be too sure what Jesus saw in these twelve men, but He was willing to extend them an invitation to do life with Him.

You may feel alone, but you don't have to be. As with the other defeater beliefs we have studied above, this belief is rooted in a lie. Suppose you can believe your loneliness is just a lie and the truth is that you are surrounded by a great company and a cloud of witnesses who are cheering you on. In that case, you can practice supernatural community before making your earthly friends.

A spirit influences this lie, and it is the spirit of rejection. Rejection is a counterfeit motherly spirit that assures your protection by cradling you in her paws of self-loathing. She will affirm your apathy while keeping your spirit drugged and lazy. She will tell you that everybody hates you and that you will never be loved. She will give you counterfeit discernment, and you will believe that people are talking about you behind your back. She will tell you that you are the special one and nobody else sees you the way she sees you. She will affirm your spiritual gifts and never allow you to use them with others. She will caress your hair while keeping a tight stranglehold of your neck. She is the spirit of rejection, and her role is to convince you that success is merely the act of sabotaging your success.

BREAKING THE POWER OF THESE LIES

We will break the power of this darkness by turning on the light of truth. In Christ, you have the authority to dismantle these defeater beliefs. We live in bondage not because we lack authority but because we lack truth and a revelation of the authority we have to use that truth to cut ourselves free.

Once you can identify the lies that are defeating you, then all you have to do is repent for believing and partnering with these lies.

Repentance is easy because it's simply asking Jesus to forgive you for believing a lie. Confess the lie, and then ask Jesus to break the power and stronghold of that lie over your mind, body, and spirit. Declare your gratefulness for the forgiveness you have received. Remember, you don't have to feel forgiven; forgiveness is yours by grace through faith in Christ alone.

So we legally state it out loud because our ears need to hear it, and so do the supernatural strongholds and entities that have reenforced the lie. Once we've declared our forgiveness, we replace the lie with the truth. And where do we get the truth? Well, we must ask the Holy Spirit. It is not just a psychological exercise in which we state the opposite of the negative. We must ask the Holy Spirit to tell us what the truth is. No matter how simple or complex, you will know the truth because God's word can support it, and so you will want to undergird the truth with whatever scripture verses the Holy Spirit reveals to you. Once you've completed this activation, you will want to export it into your journal. Write down the lie that you believed and how that lie has been impacting your life, and then write down the truth and the supporting biblical texts.

I encourage you to revisit your journal as often as you can and read it out loud, proclaiming the truth of God's word over your life and allowing your spirit to be baptized in the water of God's word. It is what we call brainwashing, and it's good because we are transformed by the renewing of our minds.

CONCLUSION

You *are* supernatural, and your entire life has been supernatural.

You have a supernatural villain who has exploited the hardships and difficulties within your past to get you to believe lies concerning the character and nature of God.

The problem is not that God has withheld the supernatural realms of heaven from you, but you have kept yourself safe by locking the door from the inside.

Trust is the key to unlocking the supernatural realms of heaven, and you are now beginning to step into the knowledge of who you really are.

The next chapter discusses the supernatural fuel needed to step into injustice and release the kingdom. I am not assuming you are somehow 100 percent fixed and ready to engage simply because you read this first chapter. Still, I hope I have given you the key to unlocking supernatural possibilities.

In the ancient Hebrew way of teaching, I end with two questions. Will you have the courage to lean into the tension of these conversations and questions? Are you willing to move on to the next chapter while allowing the Lord to continue shepherding you through the rough waters of the past?

ACTIVATION PRAYER

Dear Jesus,

Thank You for the supernatural life You have given me. I confess that my fears and doubts have locked me in, and I have allowed the lies of the enemy to cloud my understanding of who You truly are and who I truly am in You.

I declare that I am a supernatural being created in Your image, and I renounce the lies and deceptions of the enemy. I ask for Your forgiveness for not trusting You enough to unlock the supernatural realms of heaven You have prepared for me.

Lord, I ask for Your guidance as I step into the knowledge of who I really am. I pray for the supernatural boldness needed to step into injustice and release Your kingdom in this world. I acknowledge that I am not yet perfect, but I trust in Your grace and mercy to continue to shepherd me through the rough waters of the past.

I thank You for Your love, grace, and mercy, and I pray this activation prayer in the mighty name of Jesus Christ, my Lord and Savior.

Amen.

NOTES

1. Fred Rogers, *The World According to Mr. Rogers* (New York, NY: Hachette Books, 2003).

2. Kenneth S. Wuest, *Wuest's Word Studies from the Greek New Testament*, vol. 3 (Grand Rapids, MI: W.B. Eerdmans Publishing Co., 1973), 104.

CHAPTER TWO

BREAKTHROUGH FUEL

"Being brave isn't the absence of fear.
Being brave is having that fear but finding
a way through it."
—BEAR GRYLLS *God Help Us All*

Whether it was slipping into a hospital room where we were zipped up in hazmat suits to enter quarantine, driving across the border into Ukraine to minister to refugees ten weeks after the invasion, rolling up into Seattle's CHOP (Capitol Hill Organized Protest formally known as CHAZ) at eleven o'clock at night, getting gassed while leading people to Jesus in the ANTIFA protest in Portland, or like right now, I'm waiting for my religious visa to do meetings in Moscow, Russia.

But the US embassy is saying I might need to arrange for my private means to get out of the country. The most incredible thing I've ever seen is that Jesus requires fuel, a fuel I wasn't born with. When burned, fuel creates power, which is also

needed to sustain a flame. In this chapter, I will show you the critical ingredient required to make your breakthrough fuel.

It was Monday, March 2, 2020, at about 12:30 pm, and we were finishing up our soup and sandwiches and then continuing filming. The lady who leads our hospitality ministry at our church walked into the room with a worried look and said, "Did you hear the news?" I responded, "No, what's up?" She informed us that seven senior citizens had just passed from COVID-19 at a convalescent home in Kirkland, Washington. The first coronavirus fatalities in the nation. Ground zero.

Bobby Conner was sitting at the table and had just finished up three days of prophetic meetings. He spread his mouth with his lips locked tight as if trying to smile without showing his teeth, but his eyes had no smile. His eyes said to me, "Well, here we go." Five days later, on March 7, Satanists descended upon Olympia, and they were allowed into the Washington state capitol building.

They made a circle around the state seal, where they conducted a seance. Later, they walked out onto the capitol steps and formed a large pentagram with red silk. Can you say unapologetic evil?

Oddly enough, five days later, on March 12, 2020, Governor Jay Inslee issued a ban on all church gatherings in Washington state. How much do you want to bet that these same Satanists continued to gather as Christian churches shut down in the state?

That day, March 7, I was training for a half-marathon. As I ran, I worried, prayed, and asked God to speak. God told me three things, "Opportunity, opportunity, opportunity." This crisis would be an incubator for kingdom opportunities if we dared to engage the open doors of opportunity.

One week later, we received a call from our kid's private school asking us to pick up our children due to a family that had contracted the virus. The school would be shut down. The voicemail ended with the principal saying, and I swear this is true, "God help us all."

THE NOT-SO-COWARDLY LION

In L. Frank Baum's classic, *The Wizard of Oz*, we are introduced to the character the Cowardly Lion. Since lions are supposed to be "The Kings of Beasts," the lion believes that his fear makes him inadequate. He did not understand that courage meant acting in the face of fear, which he would often do. He is a fascinating character who feels shame because he thinks he lacks courage; in reality, he was quite brave.

The great pandemic did not create problems for the church; it revealed them. The church wasn't like the cowardly lion; no, quite the opposite. We had pride in our roar, courage, and bravery, but when the rubber hit the road, and our roar was needed, the immediate sound was a meow.

It turns out the cowardly lion wasn't so cowardly, yet the courageous church wasn't so courageous. And now that the "China Flu" has waned and the imminent threat lifted, the church has found her roar again, but have we learned from this experience?

THE PROBLEM

I still remember my horror as Charlie Shamp asked a lady to take the brace off her leg. She had just had surgery and was using a cart to get around. Her face cringed as people helped her take off her leg brace. I was incapable of hiding my nervous smile. My smile wasn't joy. It was an attempt to conceal the pastoral fear I felt in my heart. Some of you will know what I'm talking about when I say "pastoral fear." It's a thing, and there's nothing like it. Think about it. What would happen if Jesus didn't heal her?

This was in March of 2016, and this was an enlightening moment. It was the moment I learned that I had a problem, a virus as typical in the church as a cold. The problem was that I said I was a man of faith and believed in miracles, yet I doubted them when I saw them. And before they could even happen, my unbelief almost wanted to keep them from happening by playing it safe.

Enter Charlie Shamp—this dude doesn't play it safe. He couldn't care less about safe. The ushers took the brace off the lady's leg, at which point Charlie asked the lady to begin walking on the leg that had been recently operated on. Yes, the atmosphere was filled with expectation, shock, and horror, making for a pretty interesting atmosphere.

With each step, the lady's face cringed as ushers held her on her left and right side. Charlie assured her it was okay and to keep walking. It occurred to me that her face cringing wasn't in response to pain but rather in fear of getting hurt. Her confidence grew as Charlie continued to assure her that she would be okay. And just like that, she began walking on her foot, completely pain-free. She was healed! Now every person in the room had the faith of a healing evangelist. It was as though anybody could pray for the sick, and they'd be healed. The atmosphere was electric, but it cost something; it took one man to be brave.

Hence the problem. Andrea and I have four children, Gen Z and alpha Gen. They are among the safest generations to ever grace the planet. They wore helmets on their bikes and seat belts in the car, and they didn't wander off, not even at church (or at least that's how we instruct them).

When I was a kid, things were different. I wandered off, especially at church. I would get home, do my schoolwork, run out into the woods to build tree forts, and pretend I was Robin Hood. The rule was to get home before dark. We would ride in the back of pickup trucks and journey on our bikes a couple of miles into town to hit up the baseball card shop.

Things have changed. Things have become very safe, and that's great. Andrea and I love our kids and want them to be around for a long time. The problem isn't safety, but the children are not taught about bravery. It's not being modeled.

There is no justice without bravery, and there is no bravery if we are dictated by an eleventh commandment of "thou shalt play it safe." Peter walked on water, but he almost drowned. How unresponsible of Jesus to provoke him to step out of a boat at sea.

Jesus knew His movement would be outlawed and that most of His followers would be martyred, yet He invited them to follow Him anyway, and He never gave them a disclaimer up front as to what the cost was to be.

Less than a year later, I knew I had changed. I was at church with my family, and a lady came to the front who needed a miracle. No joke, she had the same leg brace and used the same cart to get around. Now it was my turn. I asked the lady to remove the leg brace. What was so amazing about this moment was as she pulled off her brace, there was no fear in my heart—only excitement. I had changed.

June 28, 2020

As the clock struck 10:00 pm on a balmy Sunday evening, the moon emerged from behind a veil of wispy clouds, casting its luminescence upon a scene that would soon be etched into the archives of history. With precision and skill, we maneuvered our grandiose 15-passenger van to a halt, just within the boundaries of CHOP—the Capitol Hill Organized Protest. Nestled at the juncture of Cal Anderson Park and the neighboring streets, this revolutionary zone was birthed on June 8, 2020, in the wake of George Floyd's tragic demise, as ardent protestors took up arms against the Seattle Police Department's retreat from its East Precinct building, heeding the "clarion call" of Mayor Jenny Durkan. The police department doors were left unlocked, allowing ANTIFA to quickly establish a sniper nest on the rooftop without breaking in.

David Cusick, Jeremiah Gibson, Aaron Packard, Alex Parkinson, Charlie Shamp, and I walked past the sign that welcomed us to The People's Republic of Capitol Hill. Being a resident of Seattle, I had been in this area many times, yet I had never been here before. We had entered a war zone.

A riot of colors clashed in a chaotic display on the walls as we stepped into the seedy alleyway. Graffiti was layered upon graffiti, creating an anarchic collage of protest and rebellion.

Murals of fierce resistance juxtaposed with bold slogans, each telling a story of pain and anger. The air was thick with the smell of weed and other undiscernible funk, and every window was boarded up with plywood that had become caked with layers of rebellious markings. We barely had time to take in the scene when a girl, no older than 18, ran up to us with a worried look. Her eyes darted over us, scanning our faces with suspicion as she was tasked to vet us to ensure we weren't cops. Once we revealed our identities, she let out a sigh of relief and then quickly got to the point. She informed us that women were vanishing every night, and rape was common. She begged us to keep a watchful eye and report any suspicious activity. In this lawless zone, the community had to rely on itself to police the streets.

I have had people criticize me because of the claim of rape being commonplace in CHOP. However, one CHOP volunteer, Gary, was living in the zone, not because of the political cause. He was there to be a good Samaritan. He informed us that he had personally rescued three women from being raped.

Walking through the thick, oppressive atmosphere, I stumbled upon a young man with short, tousled dreadlocks rolling a joint. But an unusual sensation washed over me as my eyes locked on to him. The Lord had highlighted him to me, a beacon of light amidst the overwhelming darkness that seemed to engulf the entire area. Praying for courage to approach him, I approached where he was leaning against a concrete construction barrier. My heart pounded with anticipation as I asked him why he was there. Without missing a beat, he launched into a passionate and articulate monologue about the cause and purpose of the movement. As he spoke, I could feel the presence of the Lord growing stronger, filling the space between us. He kept speaking until the Lord started to talk to me about him.

At a certain point, I interrupted him and asked him if I could share something with him. I told him that I felt he had been misunderstood and that people needed to hear what he was trying to say. I told him that there was a fire in his belly, and it was a fire that God had put in him. As I was speaking, he began to freak out. "How do you know that?!" He looked at his buddy, "We were just having this very conversation today!" He put out his hands and said, "Pray for me!"

We all came around him, prayed, and prophesied. That was Rio. He was the man put in charge for the final week of CHOP. Imagine that, we were now in CHOP with the blessing of CHOP leadership.

A daring figure on a motorized skateboard whizzed past me, brandishing a loaded shotgun. In the distance, a group of individuals marched down the street, their AR-15s held with conviction. One man strutted along the pavement, creating a ruckus by thrashing garbage cans with the butt of his firearm. They were all armed, strung out, and increasingly paranoid. The atmosphere was thick with speculation that the law enforcement authorities were imminent. The troops were prepared to hold their position, even those who were inebriated and unable to keep their balance, firmly believing they were ready for whatever lay ahead.

Charlie was prophesying to a young man, reading his mail, and I was keeping an eye out so Charlie could minister while CHOP foot soldiers set up a blockade and were getting ready for a shootout. I finally grabbed Charlie and said, "Dude, we got to go!"

As we made our way out, a menacing BLM Satanist with striking pentagrams etched into his face suddenly blocked our path. While he certainly looked intimidating, we didn't feel as scared as we felt bold and ready for anything. He seemed convinced that we were cops and asserted that we would still meet our demise even if we weren't. He sneered, relishing in the discomfort he caused us, declaring that he and his cohorts were killers and that we were nothing but targets. As we tried to assert ourselves, he warned that no one would bat an eye if he decided to end our lives right then and there. He made it clear there would be no help for us if we cried out, for we were no longer in the safety of the United States of America. Despite his threats, we stood our ground and refused to be intimidated. He ordered us to leave and never return, threatening that our fate would be sealed if we ignored his warning. But we didn't flinch and simply walked away, knowing we dared to face whatever lay ahead.

We were back the following day, but we never saw him again.

That night a young man was shot in CHOP. Rio placed the young man in the back of his Nissan Pathfinder and attempted to drive him to the hospital. Rio said that the first hospital refused to treat him and that cops surrounded him on a side street minutes later. He screamed at the police, "I have a young boy dying in my car." He said they didn't believe him. He grabbed the young man from the car, and pulled him out into the street. The young man had already bled out and was now dead.

The following day, the young man's father stormed back into the CHOP, brimming with rage toward the leadership. Rio aggressively stepped forward and confronted the furious man. With fervent emotion, he attempted to clarify the events that had transpired, but the father was inconsolable. His heart ached from losing his beloved son, and his grief was palpable. He was overwhelmed by helplessness and despair, and he could no longer contain his disgust. As the father retreated down the winding road, I approached him with empathy. I expressed that I would be holding him in my heart and promised to pray, hoping to offer solace in his moment of anguish. Surprisingly, he handed me his phone number, imploring me to call him in the future. Over the next few weeks, we spoke several times, and I learned more about the father's struggles and pain. He even caught the attention of Sean Hannity, who dedicated an entire show to interviewing him.

During those four days we saw miracles, salvations, deliverances, and the justice of Jesus permeate an area where law enforcement was forbidden to go. It wasn't safe, but it was what Jesus wanted.

I was changed—praying for people inside a church would never be scary again.

CHAOS

So we have determined you are unapologetically supernatural. And we have determined that your role is to execute justice, restoring the peace the villain has shattered.

Where do you belong? In the chaos! Genesis chapter 1 says that God created the heavens and the earth, and the way

He created was by the Spirit of God (the *ruach* of God) hovering amid the formless and void or, in Hebrew, "tō-hū bō-hū," pronounced *to'-hoo bo'-hoo* (Strong's H8414, H922).[1,2]

When the rabbis read the Torah, it sounds like they are saying, "Toe Hue Voe Voe Hue," and that's how I try to pronounce it. It describes the madness of the celestial chaos waters. One definition is that it is a realm that is chaotic and nonsensical. I liken it to clanging cymbals without the government of rhythm or a time signature, and when I preach on this, I beat a cymbal with a drumstick randomly, erratically, and as loud as I possibly can.

This chaotic environment is the canvas for the creation account of Genesis 1. Smack dab in the darkness and chaos, the Holy Spirit broods, and right there in the midst of His hovering, the voice of the Lord speaks, "Let there be light!"

At this point, we see seven days of Yahweh organizing the cosmos, which means order out of chaos. Therefore, creation is an act of divine justice and the establishment of peace.

So where do you belong?

In the darkness and chaos.

What are you to do?

Execute justice by restoring peace.

A NEW ERA OF ENGAGEMENT

A new dawn is emerging upon the church, calling forth a vibrant and powerful awakening from our spiritual slumber. The time has come for us to cast off the shackles of lethargy and dive into a new supernatural era noted for active engagement.

Gone are the days of cowering in fear, for we have learned that even amidst the chaos and darkness, the divine presence of Yahweh prevails. The tumultuous storm no longer fills us with dread but excites us with the prospect of divine creation on the horizon.

A crisis is not an indicator that we should retreat or hide away but rather a call to arms, an opportunity to arise and shine. We shall not be subdued by the challenges that lie ahead, but instead, we will rise up and conquer them with the indomitable spirit of Yahweh within us.

The critical fuel necessary for success in this endeavor is supernatural bravery. It is the same kind of righteous anger David, a simple shepherd boy, felt when he heard the demonic hybrid giant Goliath mocking the children of God. It is the same strength of conviction Gideon experienced when he was empowered by the Burning One. And it is the embodiment of the character and nature of Jesus, who did not shy away from the challenge of the cross and the grave but rather embraced it and emerged victorious.

Don't get me wrong; this is not an aggressive spirit, a rogue outlaw mindset where we walk around looking for a fight. It's a vigilant spirit, an assertive disposition so that when the battle comes for us, we are ready to deal with it.

When chaos rolls into your city, the church must be the first responder, whether it's a natural disaster, a political agenda, or an unruly mob. When we respond, we do not show up matching or mirroring the spirit we are up against. We subvert the demonic agenda by showing up in a contrasting, heavenly, and Holy Spirit.

The weapons of God are more powerful and overcome any demonic weapon:

> *For the weapons of our warfare are not of the flesh but have divine power to destroy strongholds. We destroy arguments and every lofty opinion raised against the knowledge of God, and take every thought captive to obey Christ, being ready to punish every disobedience, when your obedience is complete* (2 Corinthians 10:4-6 ESV).

TRUST BEFORE CONFLICT

Now we will begin to build upon the building blocks in Chapter One. Before we get stimulated by battle mode, we need to see that the foundation we build on is trust. In Yahweh we trust! It means no matter the outcome, we will trust and obey God.

Trust is not outcome-motivated, meaning we don't trust God to get what we want. We trust God so He gets what He wants. We must allow our motivation to mature so our happiness is not achieved when we get what we want, but rather when God gets what He wants.

Suppose we can build a relationship with God on a foundation of trust. In that case, trust will be able to support us when we go through hardship and conflict, yes. Still, that trust will also be our fuel for supernatural bravery, so we will voluntarily enter into it to administrate peace.

Let's make this a little more practical. Relationships can't survive if they don't have trust. Trust is the glue that keeps individuals super sticky so instead of conflict eroding the foundation of a relationship, it strengthens it.

When a marriage is built on a foundation of selfishness, the conflict must be avoided because it's just too uncomfortable and painful. Conflict is quite revealing. When you get in a fight with someone, you see a part of them that is normally hidden, and if there's insecurity and shame within that person, they will usually have to do something drastic to reassume control and cover their nakedness.

For this reason, whenever I get to work with a couple preparing for marriage, my first question is, "Tell me about your most recent fight and who won?"

If the couple says, "Oh no, pastor, we don't fight, we have the Holy Spirit, and we are above that sort of thing," I will send them on their way and tell them to return when they are ready to begin discussing marriage.

Every successful couple must learn how to fight each other in a healthy way so they can level up to use their passion to fight for each other. The goal is that the couple eventually goes back to back, and instead of using their energy to fight against each other, they use their union to engage the real enemy.

If we don't have trust, conflict can mean the end of a relationship or opportunity, but we if have taken the time to build trust, conflict can be the opportunity for greater intimacy.

In this time of awakening, some within the church are being aroused simply by militant angst, aggression, and a boisterous spirit that is disruptive but without purpose or strategy. In this era of engagement, the church is in danger of enlisting as a soldier in God's army without first saying her vows to Christ and committing to being His bride.

LOVE ENGAGES

In 1 Corinthians 13, Paul says if we don't have love, we better figure that out first before we start thinking supernatural engagement, activity, and ministry can make up for not having it. It can't.

If we don't have love, our engagement has no kingdom value. Love is what makes our ministry matter. You can engage and not have love, but you cannot have love and not engage.

Many people want to engage in a supernatural activity because they desperately want to be loved and celebrated. It is what a celebrity is; it's just a celebrated person. People seek fame because they so desperately want to be loved and celebrated. For those who finally arrive at celebrity status, it can be pretty disappointing that celebrity status usually comes with more disdain and rejection than praise and affirmation.

In the kingdom, we must ask the Father to come and love us in the areas that desire to be loved, lest our ministry efforts are motivated by lack of love instead of being motivated by love.

If we want to exploit so we will no longer feel so rejected and alone, no amount of celebration from man will ever fill that part of your heart.

A good prayer to pray is, "Father give me Your heart of love so that I can love others from Your heart."

And the test results will be seen when people try to coach or criticize you. Will you have the humility to lean into the confrontation and pursue greater understanding, relationship, and maturity, or will you flee the battleground, taking the easy and cowardly way out?

Love engages. It values the work that relationships require. Do you love your city? Do you love God's kingdom? Do you love your marriage? Do you love your children? If so, your love requires your engagement.

This is what we do. We get beaten down, humbled, and knocked on our butts, yet we always get back up, get up, and get up again. We engage, and we engage again because that's what love does. We are not in it for our comfort or the fame, but we are in it for the kingdom, and we know that buffeting produces strength and maturity.

This maturity is what slowly carves out our belief structure, and this belief structure is what slowly carves out our behaviors. It is the fruit of the Holy Spirit and happens without force. As chaos erupts, it becomes easier and easier to see the peace you could bring to the situation, and as you engage, you begin to volunteer quicker and quicker. The confidence produced from the previously resolved conflict gives you the courage to respond speedily to the next, to the point that no matter how busy you may be, you will begin to get bored when you are not responding to injustice.

JOYFUL COURAGE

In Luke 2:54-60, we see Peter deny Jesus three times, scared and embarrassed. Not looking so apostolic now. However, in Acts chapter 2, Peter is transformed by the burning fire of the Holy Spirit. He preaches the gospel of Jesus Christ quite assertively as a response to the mocking crowd, and boom, we see the birth and establishment of the apostolic church. Peter begins his sermon by defending the disorderly actions of their gathering, saying, "We are not drunk on wine, as you are assuming." Peter needed to explain that this boldness was not the result of liquid courage. "We are very filled with the Holy Ghost!" It was the result of supernatural, joyful courage!

On the fateful morning of February 24th, the Russian czar, Vladimir Putin, announced an ominous "special military operation" for the "demilitarization and denazification" of Ukraine. In the blink of an eye, the Russian invasion picked up from where it had paused several years earlier. In the aftermath, a horde of Ukrainian citizens was forced to flee their beloved homeland, braving the bitter cold and brutal weather conditions. The refugees, including entire families, were forced to stand in serpentine queues stretching for miles as they made their way to the borders in search of safety. Exhausted, dehydrated, and ravaged by sickness, many fainted. Those who survived were left traumatized, scarred by the hellish scenes they had witnessed while fleeing their small towns.

Charlie and I were together two weeks after the invasion at our Declaration Conference in Seattle. I said to Charlie, "I think we should go to Ukraine. What do you think?"

"You serious?" Charlie responded. "Yeah, we should go over there and minister to the refugees." Charlie didn't hesitate, "Let's go."

As masses desperately sought to flee the country, we were headed straight for it. In four weeks, on April 6th, I boarded Delta flight 145 bound for Amsterdam and then on to Poland. After spending two days in Poland at the refugee centers at the Poland/Ukrainian border, we embarked on two different trips into Ukraine to minister to refugees. We were warned of the dangers ahead, cautioned that we would be venturing into the "Wild West" with no one to turn to if things went awry. Yet as we crossed into Ukraine, an extraordinary sense of supernatural peace washed over our team, and our faces beamed with joy. Fueled by the Holy Spirit, we proceeded with Holy Ghost courage. We saw Jesus minister deeply to the hearts of these precious Ukrainian people. We heard stories that were tragic and hard to comprehend.

One thing was for sure: this is what we were created for—to engage, stepping into the same anointing of joyful courage that Peter stepped into in Acts 2 and to bring the shalom of heaven into the chaos.

BREAKTHROUGH FUEL

Ever since I was a child, I was moved by the scene of young David entering the war zone where his brothers were camped. David must have felt the passion of seeing his brothers and the army of God taunted by a Nephilim hybrid monster of a man, an enemy of God. Here is David, and he's a bit out of his lane. He's not a soldier, just a boy, a shepherd boy. I hear his thoughts, *Isn't somebody going to do something? How can this giant get away with this? Just because he's big and dangerous. Why should the people of God be intimidated by danger? We are God's chosen people!*

Somebody needed to do something. But nobody would. And so, the child volunteered.

You are unapologetically supernatural, and God is about to fill you with breakthrough fuel. You are going to be a first responder in the Lord's army. You may not be the biggest, the smartest, or the most famous, yet you will be the first to say, "Here I am. Send me!" You will be aware of the greatness of your authority because you will understand whose great authority you are submitted to.

You will know that nothing is impossible for our God and justice and mercy matter greatly to Him.

In James chapter 2, we see clearly that faith without works is dead. Here's what that means. Talk is cheap, and love that is only confessed verbally but without action is a sham. Jesus did not die on the cross and empower His church so we could have good church meetings. Jesus provided the breakthrough fuel needed to transform entire nations. Our insecurity and information addiction have convinced us that merely praying and watching more prophetic YouTube videos will bring the breakthrough our generation is waiting for.

The church has been bunkered up in her holy ghetto, trying to convince the people that once she is holy enough, Yahweh will send revival and kill the giants with fireballs. It isn't revivalism. Moralistic deism enables passivity and procrastination in the army of God. The church is not waiting on God. God is waiting for His children to come up and into their right minds and statuses.

- Bravery is not screaming in microphones, hiding in church buildings, and shaming men with porn addictions while standing five feet above them on an elevated platform.
- Bravery is opening your home, your life, and your heart. It is sitting down with someone struggling over a cup of burnt coffee and

pulling them out of their pit. Bravery means offering people hope, joy, and breakthrough that can be found in Jesus.

- Bravery is tears and laughter.
- Bravery is vulnerability.
- Bravery is a date night with your wife, hot chocolate with your daughter, or fishing with your son.
- Bravery is calling yourself a minister of the gospel of Jesus Christ.
- Bravery is doing what nobody else is willing to do.
- Bravery is releasing what others cannot release—a response from heaven.
- Bravery is walking in and releasing the justice of Yahweh.

In Him, you are brave.

ACTIVATION PRAYER

Jesus!

I come to You today with a desire and expectation to begin walking and living with new and profound supernatural bravery.

I know You are the source of all power and with You, nothing is impossible. I declare that I am filled with Your love, and that love, this perfect love, casts out all fear.

I declare that I trust in You, Lord, and that I am confident in Your ability to guide me through every situation that comes my way.

I declare that I have been filled with the Holy Spirit and may have the strength and courage I need to face any challenge with confidence and boldness.

I declare that I am more than a conqueror through Christ Jesus, who strengthens me. Your plans for me are good, and You have equipped me with everything I need to fulfill Your purpose for my life.

Please give me a heart of compassion and generosity for others so I may share Your love with those around me. Help me to be a light in the darkness, a beacon of hope to those who are lost and afraid.

Lord Jesus, I declare I am brave because You are with me. I trust in Your promises and know You will never leave or forsake me.

Thank You for Your love, Your mercy, and Your grace. May I always walk in the supernatural boldness made possible by Your love and the power of Your Spirit.

In Jesus' name, I pray. Amen.

NOTES

1. "Genesis 1:2 Text Analysis," Biblehub, accessed November 7, 2022, https://biblehub.com/text/genesis/1-2.htm.
2. "Ruach and the Hebrew Word for the Holy Spirit," Fellowship of Israel Related Ministries, June 12, 2021,

https://firmisrael.org/learn/the-hebrew-word-ruach
-and-gods-breath-in-our-lungs.

CHAPTER THREE

DETERMINING YOUR SUPERNATURAL TRAJECTORY

"Seekers will be finders, and finders will
be sought."
—BOBBY CONNER

THE SUPERNATURAL SIGNIFICANCE OF EATING

Yes, that's right, we are now going to talk about
eating. In the Bible, eating is a big deal, not because
food is supernatural, but because there is something radically significant about hunger. Consider
how humanity's first sin involved eating; the first
temptation was centered around food.

But don't get bummed out, because I promise
you this will not be a chapter on nutrition and the
importance of maintaining an excellent physique.
There are entire books given to that topic, written
by experts who can dive into the spirituality and
science of diet.

Isn't it curious that God put two trees in Eden's
garden? Both were fruit trees and food sources.

Consider these words.

And the Lord God commanded the man, saying, "You may surely eat of every tree of the garden, but of the tree of the knowledge of good and evil you shall not eat, for in the day that you eat of it you shall surely die" (Genesis 2:16-17 ESV).

It is assumed that the tree of life could be partaken of and would be the tree that would preserve and sustain life. Two trees—one tree would sustain, preserve, and facilitate supernatural life, while the other would supernaturally unlock the knowledge of good and evil. Here we see two trees that God personally created, and yet God and His love, in light of His long-term plan, established a boundary for His children around what could be consumed. He did not, however, place limitations on what they would desire.

Now here's where it gets fascinating. The temptation around the tree of knowledge of good and evil centered around the reality that what you ate would transform you, proving the old idiom to be correct, you are what you eat! For Lucifer to corrupt humanity, he couldn't just convince them to do something wrong but had to introduce something supernatural and foreign from the outside world into the inside of who they were. The disobedience would have to enter them; they would have to eat. The mouth is a portal to the stomach, the energy production center where food is broken down, and then the elements of the food are converted to supernatural fuel. The programming of the fruit then gets sent throughout all the neurons of the body via the gut.

Oddly enough, there are approximately 100 billion neurons in the human brain, and your gut contains 500 million neurons, which are directly connected to your brain through nerves in your nervous system.

The entire seed line of humanity could only be corrupted if the virus entered them. Adam and Eve had to eat to bring something unnatural into the body and mind, and bring it into them because what comes into the body can then transform the body from the inside out.

The serpent began his temptation sequence by getting Eve to look at the fruit to awaken desire through the eyes. Then he attempted to revive a hunger or maybe even jealousy for deeper significance and to be just as famous as Yahweh Elohim, catering to the vanity of humanity's identity. It is the reason why God hates pride with such a passion.

So Lucifer said to Adam and Eve, "Look at the fruit. Desire the fruit. Eat the fruit. If you bring it into you, it will transform you." The tree of knowledge of good and evil was not a tree of death, but death was the consequence of disobedience to God. Still, the tree itself was a tree that required maturity, a maturity that Adam and Eve did not yet possess. It is important to remember that everything God made was good, including this tree, but in essence, it provided knowledge that wasn't needed.

When we refer to the knowledge of good and evil, we are talking about a deep discernment, divine street smarts of sorts, and here Yahweh tells Adam and Eve not to eat of the tree because this knowledge, this discernment, wasn't needed. Adam and Eve had the innocence of children, and they only needed knowledge of Yahweh. Because of sin that has entered the world today, discernment is imperative, but at that time corruption had not yet entered into creation. Therefore, all they needed to do was just trust and obey God.

Genesis 3 captures Adam and Eve's transgression against the divine. They took hold of the forbidden fruit and consumed it with wild abandon. As the juices flowed into their bodies, a sensation of pure intensity surged through them, their senses fully alive with the rush of forbidden pleasure. But with this pleasure came a sudden and profound awareness, a realization that would shatter their innocence and leave them reeling. The weight of their transgression hit them with such force it was as if their very souls were broadcasting a signal of shame to the world, an unignorable beacon of guilt that could not be silenced.

This newfound awareness of their nakedness was nothing short of overwhelming, and they were filled with a sense of fear and desperation. Driven by a need to regain control over their lives, they frantically grasped for anything they could find to cover their shame and restore some semblance of dignity to their tarnished souls. They gathered leaves, weaving them together, desperately trying to conceal what could not be hidden.

But even as they struggled to hide their shame, they knew it was futile. They were exposed, vulnerable, and utterly alone in a world that suddenly seemed harsh and unforgiving. And then, like a bolt of lightning from the heavens, they heard the voice of God. He was walking in the garden, a divine presence they could feel in every fiber of their being. At that moment, they knew they were truly lost, their sins could not be hidden, and they would have to face the consequences of their actions.

So in Genesis 3:9 (ESV), God responded, *"But the Lord God called to the man and said to him, 'Where are you?'"* They were attempting to hide from God.

Indeed, the repercussions of their actions would ripple throughout time, leaving an indelible mark on the human psyche. Adam and Eve were no longer the innocent beings they had been before; they had been forever changed by the weight of their sin. A virus had been embedded into the very fabric of their consciousness, and it would spread throughout the world, infecting generation after generation with the toxic seeds of shame and fear.

For perhaps the first time in human history, anxiety took root in their hearts and minds, threatening to unravel the fragile fabric of human existence. The two imposters, shame and fear, had taken hold, their insidious grip tightening with each passing moment, and it seemed as though there was no escape from the darkness that now enveloped them.

But even in the depths of their despair, a glimmer of hope remained. For though they had sinned against the divine, they were still beloved creations of a loving God, and He would not abandon them in their hour of need. They had heard His voice in the garden, and they knew He was with them, even in their darkest moments.

And so they clung to that hope, even as they faced the consequences of their actions. For though the road ahead would be long and difficult, they knew with God by their side they could overcome even the most formidable obstacles. The virus of shame and fear may have taken hold in their hearts, but they would not let it consume them completely. They would fight, and they would prevail, for they were children of the divine, and nothing could ever change that. God did not abandon them even amid their rebellion and sin. He provided them with clothing to cover their nakedness, and He promised them that one day a Savior would come to crush the head of the serpent, the symbol of evil and temptation in the story.

This promise of a coming Redeemer is the first hint of the gospel in Genesis 3. It points forward to the ultimate act of divine mercy and redemption, when Jesus Christ would come to earth, live a sinless life, die on the cross to pay the penalty for human sin, and rise again from the dead, conquering death and offering salvation to all who believe in Him. And with the ministry of Jesus would come a new commandment—to eat of the tree of life again, this time not from a literal tree, but from His own body and blood.

Two Communions

Adam and Eve partook of the fruit in the garden, and when they did, this was a form of counterfeit communion. Lucifer basically said, "Take this fruit, desire it, receive it, eat it, and it will transform you," and it did!

> *For I received from the Lord what I also delivered to you, that the Lord Jesus on the night when he was betrayed took bread, and when he had given thanks, he broke it, and said, "This is my body, which is for you. Do this in remembrance of me." In the same way also he took the cup after supper, saying, "This cup is*

the new covenant in my blood. Do this, as often as you drink it, in remembrance of me." For as often as you eat this bread and drink the cup, you proclaim the Lord's death until he comes (1 Corinthians 11:23-26 ESV).

Jesus tells His followers they can eat from the tree of life again. He tells them that the food is His own body and blood, and He wants them to desire it, eat it, and be transformed by it. True communion, received in fellowship and community, and with supernatural consequences.

Paul indicates that there are negative ramifications if the Lord's supper is received in an unworthy manner. He continues in 1 Corinthians 11: *Whoever, therefore, eats the bread or drinks the cup of the Lord in an unworthy manner will be guilty concerning the body and blood of the Lord. Let a person examine himself, then, and so eat of the bread and drink of the cup. For anyone who eats and drinks without discerning the body eats and drinks judgment on himself. That is why many of you are weak and ill, and some have died. But if we judged ourselves truly, we would not be judged. But when we are judged by the Lord, we are disciplined so that we may not be condemned along with the world* (1 Corinthians 11:27-32 ESV).

It is a supernatural meal. Not only is it true that you are what you eat, but the state of your heart, motives, and relationships can either bless or taint your supernatural meal. If you eat from the tree of life worthily, the result will be sustained life and supernatural flourishing of the body, mind, and spirit. However, if you eat of the tree of life and there is discord or disunity among you, the very meal that would typically bring life will release death.

Isn't this wild? Both Lucifer and Jesus want you to eat! We get to choose what we will eat, but know this—it is true, you are what you eat.

YOUR FOOD SOURCE WILL DETERMINE YOUR SUPERNATURAL TRAJECTORY

The number-one factor that will determine your supernatural trajectory is your food source. We eat what we desire; therefore, our desire has a way of demining our destiny.

Do you remember Exodus 16:3 (NIV)?

> *The Israelites said to them, "If only we had died by the Lord's hand in Egypt! There we sat around pots of meat and ate all the food we wanted, but you have brought us out into this desert to starve this entire assembly to death."*

The Israelites wanted to return to slavery in Egypt because they missed the food! Just get real for a second. We all know that this has nothing to do with food. It has everything to do with hunger.

Hunger is the number-one factor that will determine your supernatural trajectory.

You will seek after that which you are hungry for. I have often heard people say that the American church lacks hunger, but that's not true. It's not that the church lacks hunger; it's that it desires the wrong food.

In John 4:31-34 (ESV), the disciples are concerned about Jesus because they feel like He needs to eat something:

Meanwhile the disciples were urging him, saying, "Rabbi, eat." But he said to them, "I have food to eat that you do not know about." So the disciples said to one another, "Has anyone brought him something to eat?" Jesus said to them, "My food is to do the will of him who sent me and to accomplish his work."

It is such an amazing text that Jesus tells His disciples, "Don't try to project your natural hunger onto Me. What satisfies Me, what I hunger for more than anything, is to do the will of My Father." The supernatural hunger of Christ was to see His Father's will accomplished, and the Father's will was that there would be justice and mercy, the gift of redemption afforded to humanity, which would require supernatural intervention.

Nowhere do we see that Jesus had a hunger for the supernatural. The supernatural in and of itself was never the desired outcome. Establishing the blueprint of the Father was the hunger of Christ; it obviously unfolded in John 17:25-26 (NLT) as Jesus concluded His prayer: *"O righteous Father, the world doesn't know you, but I do; and these disciples know you sent me. I have revealed you to them, and I will continue to do so. Then your love for me will be in them, and I will be in them."*

The hunger of Jesus framed His ministry mission, which was quite simple. The objective of Jesus' ministry was to reveal the Father, and how would this be done? Supernaturally!

THE #1 REASON BELIEVERS DO NOT SEE THE SUPERNATURAL CONSISTENTLY

A lack of hunger to reveal the Father through the supernatural ministry of the Holy Spirit is the number-one reason believers do not see the supernatural consistently.

The revelation of the Father can undoubtedly come through several means. Revelatory knowledge of God's character and nature can be experienced through the word of God, anointed teaching, or even a simple epiphany inspired sovereignly by the Holy Spirit himself.

We see a precedent established by Jesus to teach the gospel of the kingdom. So we certainly wouldn't want to diminish the critical role of inspired teaching. Yet the power of God seen through the ministry of Jesus and then echoed through the acts of the apostles also reveals the Father's heart to not just address people's mindsets but to supernaturally and immediately confront the effects that injustice, sin, and the curse have had on people's bodies.

We must not compromise the reality that the full gospel of the kingdom is a gospel of signs, wonders, miracles, salvation, and deliverance from all demonic oppression and possession. Salvation is accompanied by the gift of the Holy Spirit and the baptism of fire, the gift of speaking in tongues as evidence of that. This benefits package is proof that Jesus has risen and that we truthfully proclaim the good news of the kingdom, which is *now* at hand! We do not just preach a hypothetical philosophy that claims dominion over sin, sickness, and death.

Still, we are to live a supernatural reality that proves Jesus has judged these injustices.

If you are wondering why the supernatural is not a natural part of your life, let me inform you that if you have been filled with the Holy Spirit, then a lack of the Holy Spirit is not your problem, a lack of anointing is not your issue, neither is "more of God" the right solution. God is not a liquid or a spice. You can't just get a measuring cup and add another 1.5 cups of Holy Spirit into your spirit man.

It's not a matter of more or less of God. It is a matter of your desire.

DESIRE DETERMINES WHAT YOU ACCESS

There's a reasonable probability you now have internet access. We may not appreciate the full ramifications of such access at our fingertips because it is always there; we have become familiar with it. So most of us do not take advantage of the potential of the world wide web.

Right now, you can acquire whatever natural knowledge you might need. Right now, you could get free instruction that, if you followed it, you could make a million dollars in the next twelve months, or you could get those six-pack abs that you've always wanted, or you could even get tips to become a better spouse.

When it comes to natural knowledge, a lack of access to information is not our problem. Our problem is not a lack of access. It's what we access once we are surfing online. Our desire is what determines where we go. You might access a social media page or app if you desire interaction and community. If you desire to escape, you might stream a movie or access an online video game. If you want education, you might search with a specific question. The same thing is true in the kingdom. We have unlimited access. No limits!

We are where we are not because God has withheld good things from us. We're where we're at because our desire has determined our destination. Once this makes sense to you, you will no longer be discouraged; you will find inspiration in knowing that stepping into the fullness of who you are in Christ, into your supernatural identity, is as easy as changing your appetite.

OUT OF THE MOUTH DESIRE SPEAKS

You know what is in your heart by what is coming out of your mouth. You can discern the intensity of your hunger by how often you bring it up. Sometimes when we pray, we bring something up to the Lord just once, and then we move on with our life. It's just like when we are at the store with our kids and we pass the toy section and our kids ask for a toy; we tell him no, and then we move on, keepin' on shoppin'. When that takes place, the chances are we'll probably never see that toy again, and the truth is, most likely, my kids will never even think about that toy again. They saw it and desired it for the moment but moved on because they weren't hungry for it.

It's funny; when my kids get something in their heads, and when they *really* want something, they will continue to ask and ask and ask. My kids have made PowerPoints and conducted presentations, including graphs, statistics, and illustrations. They have even built biblical and theological arguments as to why they didn't want something but why they *needed* it.

Here's a funny example. I grew up with dogs, and Andrea did not. I always thought we might get a dog once we had a home with a big fenced-in backyard. Andrea, however, didn't care if we ever had a dog. Our current home would not work for a dog, and it didn't make sense practically. But kids aren't practical.

Our kids began working on us, and of course, it wasn't a matter of want; it was a matter of need. They needed a dog. Out of their desire, their mouths spoke. Nonstop. Asking, asking, asking all the time, and it wasn't something that Andrea and I would entertain or consider. It just didn't make sense. We would tell them that we would consider it someday if we had a bigger fenced backyard.

Well, the Lord, who doesn't seem very practical, heard about their need. When an opportunity arose for a man in our church to give us a beautiful German shepherd puppy, even though it didn't make sense, Andrea and I agreed to receive it. I still don't know if it was the best idea, but our kids accepted the desire of their hearts. They had not only declared their desire, they had spoke it out repeatedly. They carved out a realm. Now we have Moriah.

If you want to know what your real desires are, just pay attention to what's coming out of your mouth. In Matthew 12:34, Jesus said, "Out of the heart, the mouth speaks." It is 100 percent true. Not only does the mouth reveal what is in the heart—what we are hungry for—but the mouth is required to create it.

In Genesis 1, we see that creation was contingent on a declaration. The desires hosted in the heart of Yahweh were manifest once He spoke them into being. As you are awakened to your authority in Christ, your prayer life will begin to change. You go from sounding like a child who needs a puppy, to declaring something in the present that you are almost confident already exists in the Father's heart. You speak it into your world by verbally carving out a foundational dimension by which the kingdom of God can be established.

I met a mighty man of God from India who walked in signs, wonders, and miracles. He told me that he would release a series of decrees over his identity and life every morning. He had them written down on the note app on his phone. It was amazing how every morning, he would declare things like, "I'm a healer. The anointing of Christ Jesus is upon me to heal those afflicted with sickness and disease. I am a prophet. I will hear God's voice with accuracy and clarity to make the heart of God known to His people. I am an apostle. I will establish kingdom realities on the earth, so it shall be here as it is in heaven," and so on.

His declarations were not just referring to his desired actions and behaviors, kingdom goals, and things he would like to accomplish. His declarations were carving out the core of his identity. Every morning he would say, "I am _____ (fill in the blank)." His words shaped the way he saw himself, because how you see yourself will determine how you view your potential.

We have to begin to see ourselves differently if we are going to start doing the greater things that Jesus spoke about. Our understanding of our identity sets the possibilities for our future. Here's one of my favorite examples: if you believe you are an athlete, you will probably begin training like an athlete. Even if you are completely uncoordinated and not athletic, you will begin training with a vigorous approach that will probably generate unprecedented results. The belief that you are an athlete will lead to corresponding behaviors that lead to returns and influences that otherwise wouldn't have been seen. Who knows? You might even be transformed into an athlete; after all, Proverbs 23:7 (NKJV) says, "*as he thinks in his heart, so is he.*" Pay attention to this biblical principle—*out of your heart, desire speaks.*

Your words will determine your supernatural trajectory.

GOD IS USING ME!

My life was radically changed in 2010 when I experienced a massive upgrade in the supernatural and saw a considerable increase in signs, wonders, miracles, deliverances, and salvations. I want to share this with you because you may be on a similar journey, and it will bless you and your faith in believing for your supernatural upgrade.

As a new pastor, I felt frustrated and disappointed with the lack of transformation I saw in people's lives. I knew God had the power to do extraordinary things, but for some reason I wasn't experiencing it in my pastoral ministry. I started praying, declaring, and crying to God for a supernatural upgrade. It wasn't just a want but a desperate need that consumed me. Every day, I reminded God that I had to see the power of the gospel at work in my ministry. I cried out loud, "God, I need to see Your power in action! I need to see Your power in action!" I was persistent and consistent in my plea and refused to settle for anything less. My hunger for the supernatural was like a fire burning, and I was determined to see it come to fruition. The supernatural couldn't just be a luxury for me; it had to be a non-negotiable necessity.

I remember standing there with Greg Daley, my associate pastor, who had become a crucial spiritual father figure. He was telling me stories of power encounters and salvations, and I was eager to learn more. I asked him, "Greg, you must teach me your ways. I've got to see the power of the gospel at work."

Without hesitation, Greg took me out into the streets. We began knocking on doors, talking to strangers, and having a blast. I'll never forget the first door we knocked on. The woman who answered was hostile and convinced we were Mormons, even though we were dressed in blue jeans and flannels. Greg asked her if there was anything we could pray for her, and she opened up, telling us that she had fibromyalgia and was in constant pain. With her permission, Greg began to pray, and as he spoke, her expression changed. Her jaw dropped, and her eyes grew wide with amazement.

Suddenly, she interrupted him. "It's gone!" she exclaimed, almost incredulous. Greg asked, "What's gone?" She explained that all the pain in her body had disappeared. She was completely pain-free. It was like a miracle had just happened before our very eyes.

From that moment on, the woman went from being entirely disinterested in us to being eager to know everything about us. I was utterly hooked. I had just witnessed the power of the gospel, and it was nothing short of miraculous.

The next day I wanted to see what I could do without Greg. I don't recommend this, but I went out to see the power of the gospel on my own. I drove to a part of town known for drug problems and systemic poverty, and as I parked my car I saw this elderly gentleman sitting at a table on his little concrete patio, rocking back and forth in his wooden rocking chair.

I locked my car and then double-locked my car. I swallowed the lump in the back of my throat, and then, like Greg Daley, I walked right up to the guy and asked him how he was doing. He responded sarcastically, joking about almost being dead while refusing to acknowledge me. He was staring away from me at an apartment across the street, so that's what I did. He wouldn't look at me, so I didn't look at him.

I introduced myself, and he told me that his name was Chuck. I told him I was a pastor, and he replied, "Wow, I've never been visited by a pastor before." Chuck's eyes were clouded with a lifetime of pain, and as he spoke I could see the years of hardship etched on his face. He told me about his upbringing, his mom, who had a habit of bringing home various men, and about the beatings he received from them.

He spoke of the night his mom took him deep into the city, down a dark alley, and abandoned him because she didn't feel fit to be his mother any longer. I listened silently as he spoke of the war and the regrets that haunted him in his final days. Chuck was at the end of his life and didn't want to feel guilty anymore.

As I stood there, listening to Chuck's story, I couldn't help but feel a sense of compassion for him. He had been through so much in his life, and now, in his final moments, he was reaching out for something to give him peace. I knew that I had to be that source of comfort for him, to give him the solace he so desperately needed.

I asked Chuck the classic evangelism question of questions, "Chuck, I have a very important question for you. If you were to die today, do you know, for sure, that you would go to heaven?" Chuck looked at me with confusion and sadness and said, "No, I don't imagine I would."

I could sense the weight of his past weighing heavily on his heart, so I asked him if he would like his sins washed away and to receive forgiveness from Jesus. Chuck nodded and said, "Yes."

As we started praying, I saw Chuck struggling with the words. When I got to the part of the prayer, "Forgive me of all my sins," Chuck detoured from the script and responded, "But I've committed so many." At this point, tears began streaming down his face, and I couldn't help but join him in his weeping.

Holding a stranger's hand in his backyard, I struggled to finish the prayer with Chuck. When we were done, I taught him how to pray for himself. I returned in the following weeks with a Bible and different books, but despite my offer to pick him up, he never felt comfortable attending church.

Even though Chuck never made it to church, his life was forever changed, and so was mine. At that moment, I realized the power of the gospel to transform even the most broken and hopeless lives. As unique and powerful as that moment was, I continued to knock on doors and witness the power of the gospel for the rest of the day.

HUNGER FULFILLED

Let me ask you this: How hungry are you for the supernatural? *Because let me tell you, hunger is the number-one factor determining your spiritual trajectory.* Are you content with just going through the motions of Christianity, or are you hungry for more of God's power in your life?

The Bible tells us that deferred hope makes the heart sick, but a desire fulfilled is a tree of life (see Proverbs 13:12). Yet many people think Christians should spend their lives longing for satisfaction and fulfillment, always hungry and frustrated. But that's not what God wants for us! His desire is for us to live our lives completely satisfied in Him.

David wrote in Psalm 37:4 (ESV), "*Delight yourself in the Lord, and He will give you the desires of your heart.*" And Jesus said in Luke 12:32 (ESV), "*Fear not, little flock, for it is your Father's good pleasure to give you the kingdom.*" Did you catch that? It's the Father's hunger to satisfy your desires by giving you the keys to the kingdom.

If your spiritual stomach is growling for more of God, get ready because you're about to step into it. As Bobby Conner once said, "Seekers will be finders, and finders will be sought." So are you ready to satisfy your hunger for the supernatural? The kingdom is waiting for you.

WHAT ARE YOU HUNGRY FOR?

It all starts with your hunger, your desire to experience the fullness of God's goodness in your life.

So take a deep breath and ask yourself, "What am I truly hungry for?" Is it a success? Financial stability? A more profound connection with God? Write it down and don't hold back. This is your chance to speak your heart's desires into existence. Are you ready to leap? To step into your destiny and claim the promises waiting for you?

But don't stop there. Take those desires and turn them into declarations. Speak them out loud every morning and watch as they manifest in your life. And as you declare your desires, remember also to declare your identity. Who are you becoming? What is your purpose?

You have the power to pull your future into the now. Don't let fear hold you back. The only thing you should fear is complacency and settling for less than what God has planned for you. You were made for greatness, and it's time to step into that greatness.

Remember, to the degree you can see it, you can become it. So see it, declare it, and then step into it with boldness and confidence. There is more out there waiting for you, and it's time to taste and see all God has in store.

THE HUNGER WORKSHEET

Instructions:

1. Find a quiet place where you can focus.
2. Get out a journal and a pen.
3. Take a few deep breaths and ask the Holy Spirit to partner with you in this.

4. Write out your answers to the following questions.

Part 1: What Are You Hungry For?

Take a few moments to write out what you are hungry for. In your own words, what is that prayer of your heart? What is that thing that may not be practical but you absolutely need? Your list shouldn't be exhaustive, maybe just three to five things.

1. _____

2. _____

3. _____

4. _____

5. _____

Part 2: Declarations

Now, begin to frame out your declarations. Choose one or two of the things on your list and make a declaration over it. This declaration should be something that you can consistently begin making over your life every morning.

Example:

I am hungry for more of God in my life. My declaration is, "I am a seeker of God and He will satisfy my hunger. I will be filled with His presence and power every day."

1. _____

2. _____

Part 3: Identity Decrees

Make a list of identity decrees over your life. What is "the you" that you are stepping into? Could you begin to pull the future into the now? To the degree you can see it, you can become it.

Example:

> *I am stepping into my identity as a leader and influencer. I am confident in my abilities and I make a positive impact on the lives of those around me.*

1. _____

2. _____

3. _____

4. _____

5. _____

Part 4: Action Steps

Now that you have identified your hunger and made your declarations and identity decrees, what are some action steps you can take to make them a reality?

Example:

> *To fulfill my hunger for more of God, I will set aside time each morning for prayer and Bible study. I will also seek out opportunities to serve in my local church and community.*

1. _____

2. _____

3. _____

Conclusion

Remember, the only thing you should be afraid of is the contentment and passivity that would love to keep you just comfortable enough, to keep you hungry for temporal things, for natural food, merely the food of this world. There is more! It is food you know not of, and you will taste it and see it as you steward it.

ACTIVATION PRAYER

Heavenly Father, I declare my deepest desire for You and Your kingdom. I am hungry for more of You, Your presence, and more of Your love in my life. I choose not to be apathetic, tired, or distracted but to press into You with all my heart, soul, mind, and strength.

I declare that I will seek first Your kingdom and Your righteousness, knowing all these things will be added unto me (Matthew 6:33). I will not be conformed to this world but will be transformed by the renewing of my mind so I may prove what Your good, acceptable, and perfect will is (Romans 12:2).

I declare that I will delight myself in You, Lord, and You will give me the desires of my heart (Psalm 37:4). I will trust in You with all my heart and not lean on my own understanding. In all my ways, I will acknowledge You, and You will direct my paths (Proverbs 3:5-6).

I declare that I will not be satisfied with the things of this world, but will hunger and thirst for righteousness, for I know I will be filled (Matthew 5:6). I will run the race set before me with endurance, keeping my eyes fixed on Jesus, the author and finisher of my faith (Hebrews 12:1-2).

I declare that I will not be afraid to dream big dreams and to ask for the impossible, for nothing is impossible with You (Luke 1:37). I will not settle for less than Your best for my life but will press on toward the goal for the prize of the upward call of God in Christ Jesus (Philippians 3:14).

Thank You, Lord, for Your love, grace, and mercy. I trust in You and Your plans for my life. In Jesus' name, amen.

CHAPTER FOUR

HOW TO DISCERN PROPHETIC MOVEMENTS

"For though you have countless guides in Christ, you do not have many fathers. For I became your father in Christ Jesus through the gospel."
—1 CORINTHIANS 4:15 ESV

WHY DISCERNMENT MATTERS

We will discuss the importance of developing a keen sense of discernment. We will do this for our safety and sustainability and, just as important, to facilitate and nurture safe and supernatural communities.

It is essential to comprehend that the supernatural waters can get weird quickly and that good and genuine Christian supernatural communities can go bad suddenly. You might wonder, *Why would I want to be involved in something if it could go south and maybe even become evil?*

You must understand that in everything God has created, the enemy does his best to pervert and use for destruction. The fact that the supernatural can be used for selfish and manipulative means does not mean that supernatural power is evil.

I wish every supernatural equipping book written was required by its publisher to include a chapter on discernment. Not so we stir up suspicion and fear within the body of Christ, but rather so that we can teach people how to recognize immaturity, seduction, and manipulation. We need to up our vigilance in the body of Christ and do much more to protect the Bride of Christ.

There has been too much self-preservation in the church and not enough shepherds willing to speak up against the nonsense that is taking place in the name of the Holy Spirit.

Jesus warns the people with these words: *"Beware of false prophets, who come to you in sheep's clothing but inwardly are ravenous wolves"* (Matthew 7:15 ESV). Unfortunately, it would seem that only the heresy hunters and cessationists (those who oppose the supernatural in the modern-day church) tend to refer to this text. This verse is the anchor text used to throw rocks at the modern-day prophetic movement, and yet Jesus is not saying to use this text as a stone against anyone who claims to be a prophet. Should we assume that all modern-day prophets are wolves in sheep's clothing? Absolutely not! This text isn't even warning people of prophets or the gift of prophecy. Jesus is referring to the danger of false prophets.

If there is a community that should be fully committed to understanding and unpacking this text, it should be us in the prophetic community. Instead, we tend to avoid this passage of scripture since it is the stick that is often used to beat us.

Jesus begins by saying beware! This text is a warning. Yes, but it's also an invitation, an invitation to discern. Jesus says, "There will be those who come to you as prophets." It is a big deal because when we think of prophets, we immediately think of those who prophesy, which is true. Still, in a larger context, the prophets are revelatory teachers who supernaturally communicate the aspects of the kingdom and the contents of the Father's heart.

Prophets are among the most influential of all the fivefold offices (see Ephesians 4:11). The second-most influential of the offices are teachers. Most current prophets are not necessarily predicting the future as much as they conduct supernatural and revelatory teaching. With its influence, the teaching office can catalyze movements quickly. New revelatory ideas have radical gathering potential. New ideas bring understanding, and understanding is critical. Hosea 4:6 says that understanding is the cure for the poverty of the soul. Yep, Francis Bacon said it this way, "Knowledge is power."

In this text, Jesus is saying that we need to be on guard against those who are coming as supernatural teachers, those claiming they have specialized intelligence regarding the future. Let me be direct: this is not a warning against false apostles or pastors. This warning is connected with the supernatural lane of the church. If we are going to be unapologetically supernatural, then discernment must not be seen as a luxury but a necessity.

Those working, teaching, modeling, and empowering the body in the disciplines and graces of power of the Spirit must be held accountable to lead responsibly. Secret knowledge, revelatory secrets, and supernatural hacks will always be a magnet for those who are hurting and looking for help. Therefore, environments offering supernatural solutions will also forever be a magnet for wolves.

Wolves are people whose minds have been overcome by an evil principality of thought. Their helmet of salvation at some time was replaced by a helmet of depravity that catalyzes a sequence of narcissistic and harmful patterns that now govern them. Wolves are those whose conscience is seared by bitterness and rebellion, and their selfish desires enable them to harm others to achieve whatever outcome they desire.

We must learn to recognize those among us who are the most vulnerable and teach the skills needed to discern the wolves.

Who are those truly looking to minister healing, and who are those who have no problem causing harm to achieve their goals?

IT IS NOT ABOUT PROPHETIC ACCURACY

Kris Vallotton taught that a false prophet does not get a prophetic word wrong but rather is one who has an evil heart. It was sad to see the accusations made against prophets in 2020 after the election was compromised. Those who had said it was God's will for Donald Trump to be reelected were now accused of being false prophets based on their accuracy.

Vallotton points out that in Acts 21:10, the prophet Agabus prophesied that the Jews would bind Paul and hand him over to the Gentiles, but when he was bound, he was handed over to the Jews. Did this make him a "false prophet"? Nope. False prophets are not false because of accuracy; they are false because their agenda is Satanic. They are dangerous because they are attractive, look just like sheep, are convincing, and seem powerful.[1]

You can sniff out a false prophet, whether or not you have a keen spiritual gift of discernment, if you know what to look for and if you know what their desired outcome is. I will give you six red flags for false prophets so that you can easily identify their tactics when you see them.

SIX FALSE PROPHET RED FLAGS

1. Hyper Sensationalism

"Have you heard about Carlsbad Poobah?" A woman with makeup made of flour and eggs crouches down in front of you, her eyes are as wide as saucers, and her perfume smells of a mixture of Katy Perry's "Meow" fragrance mixed with frankincense essential oils and mothballs. "Poobah," she continues, "used his revelatory gifts to help the Ukrainian government find a lost nuclear tank. He shape-shifted into a bald eagle and soared above the terrain, and when he found the tank, he landed on it, turned back into his human form, and confiscated the tank by snapping the necks of the Nephilim enemy combatants."

No, Carlsbad Poobah did not do these things. Neither Ukraine nor any other country has nuclear tanks, but this lady doesn't know that. She is now an evangelist for the flavor-of-the-week false prophet who makes stuff up to deceive others.

The supernatural movement is full of such sensational stories—impossibilities bowing before the feet of Jesus. We love and celebrate these stories. They inspire us to stay hungry and to keep going after the things of the spirit. Glory stories are not in themselves the problem, if they are true. The problem exists when you begin hearing rumors of unsubstantiated claims that would have significant implications. If consequences were recorded and verified, they could be a tremendous benefit to the kingdom, but instead the details are murky, and the outcomes are larger than life.

I heard about a South African man of God in a military vehicle that hit a land mine. The vehicle blew up. Fire everywhere. God picked him up and raised him above the explosion. Everybody in the vehicle died, but God gently carried him back down to the ground. This one is a true story. He is vouched for by Heidi Baker, Randy Clark, and Bill Johnson. His stories would blow your mind. His children love Jesus. He is still married to the wife of his youth, and he is humble. The fruit of his life is tremendous joy, worship, and many falling in love with Jesus.

> *Beware of false prophets, who come to you in sheep's clothing but inwardly are ravenous wolves. You will recognize them by their fruits. Are grapes gathered from thornbushes, or figs from thistles? So, every healthy tree bears good fruit, but the diseased tree bears bad fruit. A healthy tree cannot bear bad fruit, nor can a diseased tree bear good fruit. Every tree that does not bear good fruit is cut down and thrown into the fire. Thus you will recognize them by their fruits* (Matthew 7:15-20 ESV).

A false prophet will tell you sensational stories so that you will worship them. They will tell you not to worship them, but they will allow you to do it anyway. Their stories will focus on themselves and not on the good news of the kingdom. The stories will be used to substantiate their authority. The hearers generally believe that if a person's encounter was powerful, then their revelation is likewise powerful.

When you hear about an over-the-top story that sounds too good to be true, raise a red flag, don't drink the Kool-Aid, and proceed cautiously.

2. Gnostic Sequences

If you go deep enough into the internet, you will find a miracle cure for everything. Miracle snake-oil pills that will fix you without you having to change your lifestyle. The problem with these pills is that they usually either do not work or carry a list of severe side effects with them.

This same dynamic exists in the church. If you go deep enough, you will find ministers with a supernatural sequence that can cure you of just about anything. Still, when there is no corresponding natural sequence to steward and maintain the breakthrough, one usually discovers that their breakthrough was just another gnostic fad.

Gnosticism is a heresy in church history that implies access to secret and hidden spiritual knowledge. Gnosticism elevates anything spiritual while reducing, diminishing, and villainizing anything natural. This heresy would view anything of the earth as corrupt and evil but the things of heaven and the spirit realm as good and glorious. Gnostics even went as far as to deny the physical body of Jesus, saying that He was holy because He was a spirit and not human, denying the physical crucifixion and resurrection. The continual growth of Gnosticism and its gnostic groups into the second century troubled the orthodox Christians. Gnosticism was so rampant that Irenaeus wrote a five-volume book, *On the Detection and Overthrow of the So-Called Gnosis*, commonly referred to as *Against Heresies*.

Any secret knowledge or revelation that will allow you to disconnect from earthly pain, suffering, sadness, loneliness, and despair and bring you into heavenly union, bliss, and joy while costing you nothing but a blank check is a red flag. Gnosticism offers a backdoor hack to cure anything, all by accessing the spirit world, but the spirit world is most likely not the cause of your pain. We need the Holy Spirit to hack our souls because Paul says in Romans 12:2 that our transformation is made possible by the renewal of our minds.

Here's a metaphor for you: if the hard drive on your computer needs to be repaired and your software needs updates, increasing your internet speeds will not fix your problem. When having trouble, we must address the right cause to avoid wasting money, time, and precious energy on factors that will not produce fruit. Avoid health advice from people who are not healthy, parenting advice from people who don't have kids, and dating advice from people who are not married.

Your internet speeds are not the problem. Your software and hard drive need some love and attention.

3. Screen Time Without Community

Over the years, there has been no shortage of charismatic media personalities whose teachings are guaranteed to help you be "the you" you've always wanted to be. Back in the day, you could buy VHS tapes and cassette tapes. Then it was CDs and DVDs, but now it's YouTube and access to billions of hours of revelatory content on websites.

Inspired teaching is a wonderful gift to the body of Christ and one of the quickest ways to renew our minds. One of my favorite teachers is the apostle Paul. In his day, he didn't have cameras and microphones. His media vehicle was the letters he wrote, and yet I imagine he would have courses, audiobooks, and be speaking at conferences if he were alive today.

So we all agree that revelatory teaching is essential to the body of Christ, yet we also need to discern what content we are subscribing to. James makes a serious warning to those who desire to be teachers. *"Not many of you should become teachers, my brothers, for you know that we who teach will be judged with greater strictness"* (James 3:1 ESV). Why would teachers be judged with a greater strictness?

This warning makes sense when you see that teachers have always produced followers throughout the centuries. Therefore, a teacher becomes responsible for their followers; it is where we get the idea of rabbis. If you followed a rabbi, you would follow their rules, ways, and teachings. This set of values and teachings was called their "yoke." So when Jesus said in Matthew 11:29-30 (ESV), *"Take my yoke upon you, and learn from me…. For my yoke is easy, and my burden is light,"* Jesus meant, "Listen, I'm different from all the other rabbis. I have no desire to weigh you down with heavy religious burdens. My teachings are here to lift you up, not weigh you down."

It was customary that rabbis would recruit 14-to 15-year-old young men who were finishing their education, and when they saw a young man who looked promising, they would say, "Follow me." The disciple would then leave everything he knew to emulate his rabbi, thereby taking on his yoke and becoming almost a clone of his teacher. As young men left everything to be transformed by the yoke of their rabbi, the Jewish people often said, "May you be covered with the dust of your rabbi." The blessing was an encouragement to the follower that they would follow their rabbi so closely that the dust from the road coming off the feet of the rabbi would cover the disciple.

The problem with modern discipleship is that there is no dust; everything is digital. We don't follow teachers on unpaved roads; we follow teachers on Instagram and Twitter. The problem with these pseudo-media rabbis is that the invitation to follow them is fake. The following is a click on their social media page. You will never be close enough to eat their dust. We live in an era of isolated media rabbis. Please understand I'm not talking of literal Jewish rabbis. I am referring to apostles, teachers, pastors, evangelists, and prophets who are unpacking and expounding revelation in the context of the meta-communities void of real-life interaction and responsibility.

I have seen countless people in the body of Christ deconstruct and lose their faith because they were following online gurus who were peddling their out-of-the-box ideas outside the context of a real-life community.

This is where the model of a local church can be helpful. Sure, there can be a lot of issues in churches. I am no stranger to the countless problems that can exist. The church is messy, yes, but so is family, and yet, believe it or not, there is something healthy about a messy community. The relationship that Jesus had with His disciples was messy. The situations they got themselves into were chaotic. The mess is where the message gets tested. Your theology is of no value until it's been tested by fire, and when tested by fire, you must have a family to support you and to help you process, in case there are holes in your armor.

4. Everybody Else Has a Religious Spirit (or a Demon)

Riding the thin red line of narcissism and secret, hidden knowledge will always trigger doctrinal red flags. These charismatic peddlers of mystic hacks are no strangers to accusations concerning heresy. So they develop self-defense soundbites that are angry and accusing. They attack anybody who disagrees by identifying them as having a religious spirit. Whenever I hear a teacher attacking their audience more than actually equipping and encouraging, it is always a major red flag. Defensive teachers sometimes get emotional because all their teachings are constantly being challenged. Rather than making a coherent argument and defense of the faith or their doctrine, they hurl spiritual slurs, defaming the audience and other ministers. It's a matter of saving face versus defending the Gospel of the kingdom. Their teaching exists to create a lure of mystery around their persona rather than bringing clarity to the person and character of Jesus.

The assumption projected from this form of immature and possibly incorrect teaching is that anyone who is confused or disagrees is possessed by a religious spirit. Another way of saying this is, "You have a spirit of stupid." If it's not a religious spirit, there's another demon to blame. The problem with accusing confused hearers of being possessed is that the accusers rarely demonstrate authority over the demonic realm. I once knew a minister who was always accusing people of being demon-possessed, yet the minister had never once cast a demon out of anybody. He even accused me of having a demon at one point. I humbly said, "Well then, I want it gone. Please pray for me." The dude just walked away.

Yes, people can be demon-possessed, and demons can create confusion, but be on guard for ministers who are all too comfortable accusing an audience of not understanding their revelation because of demonic interference. If you are a minister who operates this way, let me tell you, it's not that people don't understand your teaching because they are all demon-possessed. We don't understand you because you are serving a meal that isn't ready to be served.

Many of these teachers are partnering with the accuser of the brethren. As Jesus said in Matthew 12:26 (KJV), *"And if Satan cast out Satan, he is divided against himself; how shall then his kingdom stand?"* You won't see a devil casting out a devil, but you will see a devil accusing others that they have devils.

5. Bride Bashing

Another red flag in the false prophetic movement that is quite common is bride bashing. Bride bashing is typically not just a willy-nilly occasional venting against the church but is a cultural norm, an unspoken value, or even a pillar within false, counterfeit movements.

It's charismatic and often funny, but to me it is usually quite sad because it comes from an extremely charismatic and gifted individual who is hurt and bleeding all over the audience. When one uses their God-given gifts and anointings to disrespect and diminish the church of Jesus Christ, they are modeling a text-book false prophet methodology.

Because of their pride, jealousy, and rejection, they are planting the seeds of division to turn people's hearts against the church while almost demanding that this heart posture be present to be close to God. What deception! Call God your Father while cursing the church Saint Augustine described as our mother. Certainly, we can find many opportunities in church culture to make light of the silly things we do and say. We can laugh at our issues and the irony of our inconstancies. All this can be done while not defaming, reducing, and dividing the church. Bride bashing is an activity that stems from those whose hurts have hardened like a lake being frozen over from dropping temperatures, and now every word that comes forth from the minister has been marinating in bitterness.

6. Elitism

Elitism is a sin, and James commands those of the faith to never manifest partiality. "*My brothers, show no partiality as you hold the faith in our Lord Jesus Christ, the Lord of glory*" (James 2:1 ESV). *Webster's Dictionary* defines *partial* as "biased to one party; inclined to favor one party in a cause, or one side of a question, more than the other; not indifferent." To get another perspective of this text, look at William Barclay's translation of James 2:1: "*My brothers, you cannot at one and the same time believe in our glorious Lord Jesus Christ and be a snob.*" Elitism is the sin of pride and snobbery. One takes the high ground position when one believes their revelation and approach to supernatural engagement is the correct way. Everybody else is simply behind the times and religious.

Elitism is a major false prophet red flag and a good posture to stay as far away as possible. Elitism is enticing because it promises an opportunity to be a part of the crowd "in the know," but these hipster mobs are ticking time bombs. "*Pride goes before destruction, and a haughty spirit before a fall*" (Proverbs 16:18 ESV). Unless there's repentance and adoption and integration of humility, these communities are just one dispute away from the sort of division that divides and then keeps on dividing.

SATAN'S #1 COUNTERFEIT GIFTING IN THE CHURCH

In 1 Corinthians 12, we are introduced to the concept of the gifts of the Spirit, and in Ephesians 4, we are told that Jesus gives these gifts to the church. And Galatians 5:22 introduces us to the supernatural character traits that are developed through a life of intimacy with the Holy Spirit.

However, one pattern we see throughout history is that Satan always attempts to counterfeit and pervert everything good that God has created. One of these areas of distortion that many believers have never considered is how Satan attempts to counterfeit the gifts of the Spirit. Believe it or not, there is an inverted and distorted counterfeit for each of the gifts of the Spirit. Here's the thing about a counterfeit: it always looks like the real deal, but it's not real and doesn't have value. There are operations of the antichrist spirit that are at work in the church, and the number-one gift that I see distorted, perverted, and twisted is the gift of discernment.

I've been pastoring for over 14 years, and it's interesting. I am always getting dreams and prophetic warnings from all over the nation. Sometimes these dreams are in these manilla envelopes and sent to me first class, certified mail, with tracking. So my team has to sign for these dreams. Most of the time, I have yet to learn who these people are sending me their dreams. They don't come with any endorsements, references, or bios. These dream parcels are big! These big fatty word documents are so large that they can't be stapled together.

There is usually a common thread that ties all these dreams together; nine times out of ten, when I begin reading these dreams, I find they are full of warnings and accusations. It might be against me, our church, the government, or another leader in the body of Christ. If I didn't have a true gift of discernment and a healthy relationship with Jesus, I might believe the warnings in these dreams. If I choose to accept them, at this point, I am choosing to allow the seed of subversion to enter my heart.

Yes, you guessed it—if you honor a false prophet, you get an impartation from a false prophet. If I chose to do this, all of a sudden, I would have an impartation of the counterfeit gift of discernment, which is the spirit of suspicion. Now I would begin to see myself, my team, my church, and other leaders differently. I may not be able to trust leaders in my network. The fruit of this "discerning dream" or warning dream won't be my fruitfulness and sharpening of kingdom effectiveness, but rather a closed heart and a closed mind.

Counterfeit discernment is the demonic spirit of suspicion and is Satan's number-one counterfeit gift at work within the church.

"From now on, therefore, we regard no one according to the flesh. Even though we once regarded Christ according to the flesh, we regard him thus no longer" (2 Corinthians 5:16 ESV). Paul is telling the church of Corinth to stop applying their worldly filters and suspicious judgment against each other and start seeing each other from the Father's perspective. You are a new creation because the old you is dead. You are a new you, a reconciled you.

The true spirit of discernment can see the truth through the filter of the blood of Jesus. It discerns the good when nobody else can. It sees the seed of light when the darkness blinds everybody else. True discernment is Barnabas genuinely seeing the converted Paul and vouching for him when the church wanted to reject him because they discerned him to be an imposter.

Much emphasis is placed on seeing in the spirit and hearing the voice of the Lord, but more emphasis is needed on smelling in the spirit. We need the spiritual gift of smell restored to the church. The ability to discern what is worthy of being eaten versus what should be thrown out because the charismatic church keeps eating the wrong stuff these days.

While on Patmos, John heard a loud voice that sounded like a song of triumph.

> *Then I heard a loud voice in heaven, saying, "Now the salvation, and the power, and the kingdom (dominion, reign) of our God, and the authority of His Christ have come; for the accuser of our [believing] brothers and sisters has been thrown down [at last], he who accuses them and keeps bringing charges [of sinful behavior] against them before our God day and night"* (Revelation 12:10 AMP).

Here we see Satan is referred to as the Master Blogger of the second heaven. He writes articles against all the Lord's beloved every day and night. True stories. Scandals of their past. Insights into the fleshly nature of God's beloved. Satan has tricked the church into thinking that this counterfeit discernment will preserve the church of the last days. The lie of the enemy is this: "Your fear is protecting you."

The truth is that the enemy is a liar. You are not safer because you are afraid. Fear doesn't make you wise; it makes you stupid. In Matthew 1:19, Joseph became worried because the potential scandal of being married to a pregnant "virgin" was more than he could handle. You can bet that the enemy did his best to bring an accusation against Mary to Joseph.

And Joseph became terrified and almost made a foolish decision, but God subdued Joseph's fear with a dream. The dream righteously judged Joseph's fear and brought him the peace and courage he needed to be the husband Mary needed and the father that Jesus would need.

Fear will compromise you by filtering what you see, turning shadows into monsters and molehills into mountains. Fear will assure you that it is wisdom and is here to help you, protect you, and sustain you. Fear tries to convince you that survival is the win, but merely surviving is no different than slowly dying.

The work of the devious enemy did not deceive Jesus but He countered the enemy's work with life. *"The thief comes only to steal and kill and destroy. I came that they may have life and have it abundantly"* (John 10:10 ESV).

Jesus modeled the abundant life by living a fear-free life. Never once did He live in fear of the enemy, and He never feared losing His life. Jesus wasn't interested in surviving and was never afraid of anyone taking His life. Nobody could take His life because He had already given His life.

Jesus never walked in suspicion, for His heart was open to the compromised, the sinner, and even the liar. As seen in the story of the woman at the well, a woman who thought she could theologically maneuver around Jesus' discernment, yet He picked up on what was going on. His discernment didn't lead to rejection but rather interrupted the pattern to get past her defenses, which worked. She opened her heart to Him, but in reality Jesus knew the secrets and compromises of her heart, yet He loved her and received her despite her brokenness and sinfulness. We have so much to learn from Jesus.

Suspicion is not discernment; it's demonic, leading to rejection and isolation, which is fear-based and poisons our dreams, prophetic words, and decisions.

Leaders who constantly trigger suspicion and fill people's hearts with fear are a major red flag. You do not need to fear deception, demons, or even false prophets. True discernment drives out all fear and gives you the courage to connect with others in love and grace.

"There is no fear in love, but perfect love casts out fear. For fear has to do with punishment, and whoever fears has not been perfected in love" (1 John 4:18 ESV). True discernment has nothing to do with fear and everything to do with the character and nature of God as a good and faithful shepherd.

We don't fear wolves, we don't fear principalities and powers, and we don't fear man—*we fear God!*

BREAKING THE POWER OF FALSE MASTERS

We received a phone call at the church from a woman being tormented by a "spiritual advisor" from her past. At night this person would appear in her room and take possession of her body. She felt she had no authority over this person and had sought out deliverance ministry from some tremendous ministers within the body of Christ.

When she reached out to us, I felt underqualified to deal with something so severe. I reached out to a minister in our region who had quite a bit more experience in this sort of thing—Apostle Tom Cornell—and for about an hour, he equipped me with the tools needed to break the power this false master had over this woman.

As we began to take her through deliverance, there were demonic spirits that had to come out of her first. The Holy Spirit revealed what these were to the woman as we prayed. Once she had confessed her sins and closed the doors (see my book *Pattern Interrupt* for more on closing the doors to demons), the Lord revealed to me that she had a soul tie with this person who had given her spiritual consulting in the past.

A soul tie is an attachment when we allow our souls to unite with one another. It is usually referred to as a uniting of souls through sexual engagement. In 1 Corinthians 6:16, Paul says that one who gives themselves to a prostitute becomes one flesh with that prostitute. Paul says that sex creates a bonding or a unifying of the body, soul, and spirit.

In the occult, sex is used as a technology to merge or unify souls and spirits. However, it is a perversion and hacking of God's original technology. God created sex to bond and unify a woman and man within the context of covenant marriage. This act of love is an act of worship, and it is supernatural and holy. Throughout the Old Testament, sex was referred to as "knowing" because, during a moment of true intimacy, two people submit their wills, emotions, feelings, imaginations, and bodies to each other.

Sex, however, is not the only way a soul tie can be established. You can give yourself to a person or even an organization or group or idea without it being sexual. However, in giving yourself, this thing you are giving yourself to can fill the seat of intimacy that normally sex would fulfill.

The enemy will use anything or anyone he can to fill this seat of intimacy. Those demonically taught in the art of seduction and deception will exploit people's neediness to fill that seat. If the connection of the soul isn't sexual or is with a church, cult, or business organization (and yes, some businesses exploit this principle to take advantage of their employees and clients), I tend to call this a soul attachment versus a soul tie.

These attachments can be quickly and legally broken. Breaking these attachments is final, but your freedom must be guarded through healthy boundaries and not flirting, not even for a moment, with the memories or the entities themselves.

Remember, Jesus is the good shepherd, a good master who can be trusted. Every other master is a counterfeit shepherd and a gateway into disaster. To break these soul attachments, we must begin with repenting for idolatry—idolatry is the sin of giving ourselves to idols—an idol is anything we worship/fear that is not Jesus.

In fact, let's try it. Let us break the power of every false master in our lives and give ourselves entirely to Jesus, abiding in Him and He in us. His kingdom of righteousness, peace, and joy will be the realm and dominant atmosphere from which we function.

BREAKING SOUL ATTACHMENTS/SOUL TIES PRAYER WORKSHEET

Step 1: Confession and Declaration

- Begin by confessing with your mouth and believing in your heart that Jesus died on the cross for your sins and declaring His lordship over your life.
- Thank Jesus for breaking the power of iniquity, sin, addiction, infirmity, sickness, and disease over your life.
- Declare that His blood covers you from head to toe, inside and out.

- Ask Jesus to open the books of your ancestral record and declare the breaking of every generational curse going back to Adam.
- Declare that you stand before Him loved, forgiven, and free.

Step 2: Breaking Ungodly Soul Ties

- Ask Jesus to break every ungodly soul tie and ungodly soul attachment between you and the person, cult, church, business group, or religious group you are seeking to break ties with. Write the name of the person/people or group(s) in the blanks:

1. _____

2. _____

3. _____

Ask for the parts of your soul that you gave to the person(s), cult, church, business group, or religious group to be returned to you, and for the parts of their soul that you have retained to be loosed and returned to them.

- Declare that you belong to Jesus and not to the person you are breaking ties with, and that they have no power over you from this point forward.
- Ask Jesus to fill the place that the person has occupied in your soul with His love and acceptance, and to be the lover of your soul.

> By faith, declare that you are loved, accepted, cherished, and valued by Jesus.

Step 3: Closing Prayer

> Close the prayer "in Jesus' name, amen."

Note: You can repeat this prayer as many times as needed for complete freedom from ungodly soul ties. You can also seek the help of a trusted pastor, spiritual mentor, or counselor for additional support.

ACTIVATION PRAYER: BE FREE FROM A SPIRIT OF SUSPICION/FEAR

Dear Jesus,

I approach Your throne with a heart of gratitude and thanksgiving, acknowledging that You are the source of all life and the author of my salvation. I confess that I have been partnering with the spirit of fear, suspicion, and accusation, and I recognize that these spirits are not of You. Therefore, I renounce them now in the mighty name of Jesus.

Lord, I repent for my actions and attitudes that have given these spirits a foothold in my life. I ask for Your forgiveness, knowing that Your grace and mercy are freely given to all who come to You with a repentant heart.

By faith, I declare that I am forgiven, and I receive Your healing and restoration in every area of my life.

Jesus, I ask that You would judge the spirit of fear, suspicion, and accusation on my behalf. I ask that You would bind these spirits and cast them out of my life, sending them to the pit where they belong.

I declare that I am free from the spirit of fear, suspicion, and accusation. I am covered by the blood of Jesus, and I walk in the power of the Holy Spirit.

Thank You, Jesus, for setting me free. I give You all the glory and honor, now and forever. Amen.

NOTE

1. Kris Vallotton, "What a False Prophet Is, and How Not to Become One," November 21, 2020, https://www.krisvallotton.com/what-a-false-prophet-is-and-how-not-to-become-one.

CHAPTER FIVE

FOUNDATION FOR SUPERNATURAL IDENTITY AND DESTINY

"For where two or three gather in my name, there am I with them."

—MATTHEW 18:20 NIV

START WITH A FOUNDATION

As a supernatural being, you were created to glorify God by revealing His plan of redemption and restoration to the world. You have the desire, ingredients, and the Father's blessing, but perhaps you need more supernatural momentum.

Let me use the analogy of building a home to illustrate the importance of having a solid foundation. My wife Andrea and I recently started building a new home for our family. Due to the pandemic, it took over two years to get the necessary permits. Once we received the permits, the tractors came in and began clearing the land and

digging the hole where our house would stand. We could see where the foundation would be placed. After pouring the concrete and laying the foundation, everything else was built upon it, and the construction progressed quickly.

The truth is, without a foundation there can be no construction, building up, or momentum. Without a foundation, all you have are dreams and plans. With a bit of sarcasm, Henry David Thoreau said, "If you have built castles in the air, your work need not be lost; that is where they should be. Now put the foundations under them."

Sadly, I have observed that many believers need to build something but have yet to discover the importance of beginning with a proper foundation. They are just talking about what they plan to build someday—the book they want to write, the people they want to minister to, and so on. If you have big kingdom dreams and prophetic words but are not seeing any progress or forward movement, there is likely a reason for this. You must have a strong foundation to build anything of significance.

Building a solid foundation is crucial, and it takes time and effort. Take your time to start building by first laying a solid foundation. Take the time to seek God's guidance and build upon the rock of His word. With a strong foundation, you can build confidently, knowing your work will stand the test of time.

THE FOUNDATION FOR PENTECOST

In Acts 2, we witness a gathering of 120 individuals who had assembled in obedience to Jesus' commandment to remain as one until they received the gift of the Holy Spirit. Their commitment to obey Jesus by gathering, uniting, and waiting formed the foundation for the outpouring of the Holy Spirit. This community, united in heart and mind, created the perfect environment for the Holy Spirit to descend upon them like a mighty rushing wind from heaven.

This chapter highlights the importance of corporate Christianity in its proper, vibrant, and supernatural form. The principle of two or more individuals coming together isn't just a kingdom ideal but a law that unlocks growth and fruit in the lives of those who discover it. Once this key is understood, it can lead to unprecedented revelation and power in one's life and a decision never to isolate oneself again.

To begin this journey, we travel back a hundred years to the Azusa Street Revival, which birthed modern-day Pentecostalism. The foundation of this revival was built on the principles of unity, gathering, and waiting, which led to a nation-transforming movement.

In 1906, the world stood on the brink of the most significant move of God since the book of Acts. A one-eyed Black minister, William Seymour, preached a controversial message throughout Los Angeles. He taught that signs, wonders, and miracles were still prevalent, and speaking in tongues was evidence of being filled with the Holy Spirit. Ironically, he had not yet spoken in tongues himself.

Seymour initially struggled to find a place to preach or sleep due to his radical message's lack of acceptance. However, in February of that year, the Asberys offered him a stay at 214 North Bonnie Brae Street. They started hosting meetings that consisted of hours of prayer and seeking the Holy Spirit to descend upon them, like in Acts 2. And the Holy Spirit came! As people gathered in this humble abode, the Lord gathered among them. The house soon overflowed with people, and they called it "Pentecost Restored." Azusa was signified by the reenactment of the apostles' experiences in Acts 2. It was signified by the baptism of the Holy Spirit accompanied by speaking in tongues.

People would drop to their knees and speak in tongues as the Holy Spirit filled them. They spent hours in worship, experiencing visions and trances. They began prophesying and preaching as they were filled with the Holy Spirit. Every day, people were saved, delivered, and healed. The Asberys' front porch became the pulpit and the street, the pews, as Seymour preached the gospel. One day, the weight of the crowd caused the front porch to collapse, prompting the meetings to relocate to a larger space that could accommodate the crowds: 312 Azusa Street.

COMMUNITY IS THE FOUNDATION FOR KINGDOM

Whenever there is a significant move of the Spirit on earth, it is always established on a foundation of two or more gathered together. There are countless examples throughout revival history of how God uses communities of people to birth kingdom movements on earth. The Bible also contains numerous examples demonstrating the community's power in advancing God's mission. From Adam and Eve living together in Eden to the Israelites journeying through the desert and encountering God's presence to Jesus walking and working with twelve disciples and sending them out to spread the gospel, community is the precedent for heaven's establishment.

Despite the importance of community for advancing God's kingdom, it is also a tool the enemy can use to create and sustain darkness on earth. The enemy counterfeits the power of supernatural communities by creating false communities based on manipulation, control, and division. These communities are often driven by selfish ambition and a desire for power rather than a commitment to God's mission.

However, by harnessing the power of authentic community, believers can support one another spiritually and become instruments of shalom and justice. Together, they can bring heaven to earth and accomplish things that would otherwise be impossible. As followers of Christ, we must recognize the importance of community and work together to establish God's kingdom on earth.

THE PLACE WHERE NOTHING WAS IMPOSSIBLE

The story of the tower of Babel in Genesis 11 provides a powerful and cautionary lesson on the immense power and strength that comes from unifying as a community. The tower was intended to serve as a portal for humanity to access the realm of the gods and for the gods to enter the realm of man. However, the consequences would have been catastrophic and could have led to an even worse state of affairs than before the flood. Therefore, God had to intervene.

So Genesis 11:5-6 (ESV) describes it:

And the Lord came down to see the city and the tower, which the children of man had built. And the Lord said, "Behold, they are one people, and they have all one language, and this is only the beginning of what they will do. And nothing that they propose to do will now be impossible for them."

Unity can lead to the accomplishment of great things. However, God intervened to disrupt this tight-knit community by engaging it with His triune nature. He disrupted the community of man by involving the community of God. In verse 7 (ESV), God said, *"Come, let us go down and there confuse their language, so that they may not understand one another's speech."*

God scattered humanity worldwide by scrambling their speech, replacing their disposition of unity and connection with a curse of misunderstanding. It is a vital lesson for us today, for the possibilities are endless when we come together around a shared mission. When we are unified, there are no limits. When people join forces for good, whether financially, socially, or artistically, they create incredible opportunities for progress and growth that would have been impossible otherwise. When people join forces for the kingdom of God, God commands a blessing!

The tower of Babel exposes the universal law of a community. Regardless of whether one's motivations are virtuous or scandalous, the possibilities are infinite when people reach an agreement.

THE SUPERNATURAL JOURNEY CAN BECOME LONELY

I wanted to take the time to explain why building value for a community and integrating into an excellent apostolic church is crucial when exploring the supernatural. Without this foundation, becoming isolated and lonely on your journey is easy. To truly walk in the power of God and experience radical supernatural encounters, we must understand the importance of the secret place.

Recently, my church in Seattle conducted a long-term study of Christian mystics and desert fathers. We discovered this movement responded to the original apostolic church being hijacked and turned into an institutional machine. Some Jesus lovers did not rebel against these changes but did not want to be part of the performance culture, so they sought isolation and seclusion in the wilderness, caves, and forests. For hundreds of years, Christ seekers fled the circus and sought lives of devotion and communion with God, resulting in unprecedented supernatural encounters.

This seclusion was a strategy to develop intimacy with God, and Jesus modeled this principle by often disappearing to be alone with His Father. In Matthew 6:5-8, He instructed His disciples to go into their rooms, shut the door, and pray to their Father in secret.

However, these hermits were only partially isolated. They were social and hospitable, frequently visiting monasteries to share their revelations and offer impartation. They cultivated a secret-place intimacy dynamic with God as a safeguard against the Roman religious machine of their day and created a counterculture that contributed to generations to come.

It's important to remember that attacking the church is not the solution. We must guard our hearts, love the Lord, and love His people. Walking in the most excellent way, as unpacked in 1

Corinthians 13, positions us to awaken further to our sonship and inheritance without causing harm to others.

AGREEMENT, ACCESS, AND RELATIONSHIP

When engaging with the spirit realm, many methods in the occult require the participation of two or more people. For example, with the Ouija board, participants use a planchette to communicate with spirits and supernatural entities from another realm. The same goes for seances, where a group of people comes together to communicate with the spirits of the dead. In a seance, a medium often serves as a channel between the living and the dead and may relay messages from the spirits.

A noteworthy and eerie historical fact is that Mary Todd Lincoln, the wife of Abraham Lincoln, reportedly held at least eight seances in the White House. It is rumored that Honest Abe himself attended some of them. During these seances, Mary claimed to have communicated with two spirits who identified themselves as her deceased sons. They allegedly continued to visit her at night, eventually leading to their haunting of the White House. Following Abraham's death, Mary attempted to contact him through a group seance, and it was later claimed that a photograph had captured his spirit. Many people believe that the Lincoln family, along with other spirits, still haunt the White House to this day.

When it comes to the supernatural and the spirit realm, certain things can only be established when there are two or more gathered. When Jesus mentioned this, He spoke of being gathered together in His name. When we gather in His name, He is present with us. It is a major key! Coming together in the authority of Jesus Christ allows us to tap into something much larger than ourselves. When we engage the Spirit of Christ Jesus together, we step into a heavenly realm that transcends physical boundaries. A unified community that engages with Christ catalyzes a dynamic that permeates the atmosphere and impacts everyone present.

The power of Christ-centered unity can transform cities and nations. When two or three are gathered in agreement, there is a kingdom energy at work that has the potential to land the kingdom of heaven on earth. An agreement is expressed in John 17, where Jesus prays for the unity and protection of His disciples and all believers. He emphasizes the importance of unity among His followers, praying they would be one just as He and the Father are.

The difference between the Christian community and the kind of community practiced in paganism lies in the closeness, intimacy, and connection modeled by Jesus with His Father. Jesus prayed that His followers would likewise model that same form of closeness in a relationship, not just as a unified community but as a unified family.

A sincere relationship is essential for a genuine kingdom community. We see this in John 17 when Jesus expresses His love for all of us and His desire for us to experience joy, be protected from the evil one, and be set apart by truth.

As we embark on our supernatural quest, we must learn to carve out a value for an intimate connection with the Lord and a genuine relationship with each other, for we are not empowered to advance the kingdom in isolation, apart from the body of Christ, but together in the authority of Jesus Christ.

GETTING STARTED

To fully embrace the supernatural, you must find a community that does the same. That's where the church comes in. According to the New Testament, the church is the central body through which Christ carries out His mission. From Acts 2, we see that the church is meant to equip and empower believers to make disciples and demonstrate the power of God.

The Jerusalem and Antioch models for apostolic ministry provide an example of communities equipping and empowering the people of God to make disciples of nations, by proclaiming the gospel of the kingdom and walking in demonstrations of power. You can use Acts 2 as a blueprint to discover the right wineskin by which your giftings and assignments can be activated.

Acts 2 unfolds the purposes and operations of the church, beginning with a glimpse of the deep covenant community of believers. In Acts 2:42-47, the early Christians lived together and shared everything they had except their toothbrushes. They devoted themselves to the apostles' teaching, fellowship, bread-breaking, and prayer. Their love for Jesus united them and fueled their love and practical support for one another.

Second, the church served as a place of worship. The early Christians would gather daily in the temple courts and their homes to praise God, sing, dance, and rejoice in the Lord. They did this with joy and sincerity of heart. Today, the church continues to exist as a place of worship. Christians come together to praise and worship God, give thanks, study the word of God, and honor the finished work of the cross through the partaking of communion.

All of this is worship, not just the singing part. It is impossible to be unapologetically supernatural and not be a worshiper.

Third, the church serves as a vehicle of evangelism. In Acts 2:38-41, Peter preached the gospel to the crowds gathered in Jerusalem, and many people were baptized and added to the church. Today, the church continues to serve as a platform for the gospel of Jesus Christ. Missiologists tell us that planting new churches is one of the most effective ways to make disciples. Through preaching, teaching, and outreach strategies, the church reaches out to those who have not heard the gospel and invites them to join the supernatural community of believers.

Finally, the church serves as a place of service. In Acts 2:44-45, the early Christians sold their possessions and gave them to those in need. They cared for the poor, the sick, and the marginalized.

Today, the church continues to serve as a place of service. Christians are called to love their neighbors as themselves, and the church provides opportunities to put this love into action. Through generosity, partnership with other ministries, missions, and practical service, the church reaches out to those in need and demonstrates the love of Christ to the world.

Here is how the body of Christ should appear. A literal fellowship of like-hearted people who love God and love others. This body of people put the love of God into action through their faith and obedience to God. It is not something that can be accomplished by watching services on YouTube.

Digital membership to a supernatural directory certainly doesn't achieve the biblical purposes of the church. Equipping the saints for works of ministry is not the purpose of the church. That is the purpose of the fivefold ministry. For the church to be the church, real people have to engage with real people. Two or more are gathered together, not watching a replay of the week before or five years prior.

THE BIBLICAL OPERATION OF THE CHURCH

To truly love, we must first receive love. To effectively receive others, we must first experience what it means to be received. Before we can restore others, we must first be restored ourselves. We can only give it if we have first received it.

Consider a scenario where you must rescue a large group of drowning people. If you have a boat but do not know how to use it, or if you know someone with a boat but they are too busy to rescue drowning victims, you will not be able to save them effectively.

Similarly, we must understand the calling of the church before committing to engage with one. Once we find an unapologetically supernatural church that aligns with the Great Commission of Jesus Christ, we can partner to receive others.

The ministry of Jesus and the early church focused on seeking, saving, developing, equipping, and empowering those who were lost. As the lost became found, they became the ones seeking out the lost. It is because the kingdom of God is extroverted, and we are called to actively seek out those who need rescuing.

Supernatural enlightenment has never been the goal of the church. Instead, it has always been a byproduct of a relationship with God. Engaging with the kingdom realm is not the church's primary purpose. Our role is to encounter the Father and then lead as many people as possible into the good news of sonship through the proclamation of the gospel and a supernatural demonstration of the power of King Jesus.

USING THE PRINCIPLE OF TENSION IN FINDING A CHURCH

Tension, which is the principle of being stretched tight, is a principle that can be used to help you find a solid apostolic platform that will enable you to discover your identity and destiny in Jesus Christ. Tension is created when we must govern or manage two or more opposing factors or ideas. However, many Christians cannot handle tension and view it as the absence of peace. You'll recognize this when people say, "I'm sorry, I don't have peace about that." They are saying that they recognize a tension that makes them uncomfortable. Tension is often awkward, but in the kingdom, tension is essential for the health and holiness of the church.

The Lord has built tension into His church, and He has given the church five roles to not only create this tension but to hold it. These roles are collectively known as the fivefold ministry and are described in Ephesians 4:11-13. They include apostles, prophets, evangelists, pastors, and teachers. These ministry roles exist to equip the saints for doing the work of ministry and building up the body of Christ.

So how does the fivefold ministry help to keep a healthy tension within the church?

1. Promoting Diversity and Unity

One of the critical aspects of the fivefold ministry is it recognizes and values the diversity of gifts and callings within the church. Each of the five ministries brings a unique perspective and skillset, which is necessary for the church to function effectively.

However, this diversity outside of the power of the Holy Spirit can lead to division.

By acknowledging and valuing each of the five functions, the church can work toward unity while allowing for various values and methods. It helps create a healthy tension within the church, where different perspectives and approaches are valued and respected, creating movement.

2. Encouraging Accountability

Another critical aspect of the fivefold ministry is it promotes accountability within the church. Each of the five functions has a specific role, and each ministry is accountable to the others. It helps to prevent any one operation from gobbling up the others. By working together and holding each other accountable, the church can ensure it is fulfilling its supernatural mission. This accountability helps to create a healthy tension within the church, where each ministry is focused on serving God and others, rather than seeking its own agenda.

3. Promoting Growth and Maturity

The fivefold ministry is intended to equip the saints and build up the body of Christ. This means the church is constantly growing and maturing as each function fulfills its role. Growth and maturity are needed to help prevent stagnation and complacency within the church. One way of evaluating the health of a church is to find out if it's growing.

Healthy things grow. By valuing and utilizing each of the five ministries, the church can continue to grow and develop in its mission to serve God and others.

This helps to create a healthy tension within the church, where there is a constant push toward growth and maturity.

4. Providing a Balanced Perspective

Each of the fivefold functions brings a unique perspective to the church. The apostle brings a vision for the church, the prophet brings a message from God, the evangelist brings a heart for the lost, the pastor brings care and nurturing, and the teacher brings understanding and wisdom.

Together, these perspectives provide a balanced approach to ministry. It prevents any one perspective from becoming too dominant or extreme and ensures that the church serves God and others in a well-rounded way. It helps to create a healthy tension within the church, where different perspectives are valued and respected.

WHEN FIVEFOLD FAILS

During times of spiritual renewal and revival, the Holy Spirit stirs a deep understanding within people's hearts regarding their spiritual gifts, callings, and assignments. When individuals fulfill their God-given purpose, grace enables them to unite, transforming the church into a mighty river of power and possibility.

However, when human interference disrupts the movement of the Spirit, the church's dynamic changes, and the once-mighty river slows down and branches out into numerous trickling streams that lack the vibrancy and diversity of the kingdom. These streams become sects, causing and even creating divisions and denominations, leading to apostolic churches, prophetic churches, community churches, outreach churches, and Bible churches.

While there is nothing wrong with a one-lane church, ensuring you are called to that specific lane is essential. If you are, you will be content and fulfilled. However, if you are not, attempting to change the church's direction to align with your beliefs can be unproductive and harmful.

It is common for believers to try to convert their non-supernatural pastors by persistently sharing supernatural YouTube videos or attempting to manipulate their leaders. However, such actions can be detrimental and indicate a lack of trust in God's sovereign plan for His church. Changing the church to align with your preferences is akin to trying to change your DNA—an impossible task.

If you find yourself in a church that is not your calling, pray for guidance and direction, and seek out a community that aligns with your calling. Instead of trying to change the church, step into your lane and fulfill your God-given purpose.

HOW TO FIND A GOOD CHURCH

Check Their Beliefs

Before you visit a church, check out their beliefs online. You may want to use this checklist to evaulate a church.

1. ## Baptism in the Holy Spirit

   You will want to find a church that believes in the baptism in the Holy Spirit as a distinct experience from salvation, in which believers are filled with the Holy Spirit and receive the spiritual gift of speaking in tongues.

2. ## Spiritual Gifts

   Belief in the continuation of spiritual gifts as described in the New Testament, including prophecy, healing, speaking in tongues, and interpretation of tongues.

3. ## Worship

   As we have learned, worshiping Jesus together is essential to the flourishing of the believer. Believers not part of a vibrant corporate worship gathering find themselves withering about 88 percent of the time. You will want to find a church strongly emphasizing expressive, participatory worship that welcomes singing, clapping, dancing, and maybe even flag-waving.

4. ## Power Evangelism

   Find a church passionate about power evangelism,

believing in the importance of demonstrating the power of the gospel outside the church walls and in spreading the gospel of the kingdom to the entire world.

5. Authority of the Bible

Find a church that believes in the authority of the Bible as the inspired word of God and relies on it as the basis for their beliefs and practices. A pastor has struck out if he doesn't read from the Bible within the first twenty minutes of his message, three sermons in a row. I don't care how famous the dude is; find a church where the sermon finds its authority in the word of God and not based on how many likes they have on Instagram.

6. Healing

Jesus died for the forgiveness of sins and healing, and so healing is a big deal to Jesus. Find a church that believes in the power of God to heal physical and emotional ailments through prayer and faith.

7. Encounter

We are saved by grace through faith in Jesus Christ; yes, faith is essential, but according to the entire New Testament, so is encounter. Find a church that places value on encountering the Holy Spirit.

Yes, there are a hundred other things that I could mention, important things, but this will get you started.

Worship Style

Does this one even need to be mentioned? Probably. When considering a church, ensure the worship aligns with your supernatural core values. There is so much diversity within modern-day worship, and it's extraordinary. Don't be too picky, but use discernment. Can you feel the Holy Spirit when you worship? Do you sense the nearness of God? No matter how impressive the guitar or drum solos are, never compromise on the presence of God for outstanding performance. The presence of God must always come first.

Community

Find a church with a strong sense of community. Do they have home groups? Do they have a home group near you? Do they have Bible studies or other opportunities to connect with others? Here's an interesting observation you should make—after a service, do people linger and converse? Does it seem like they enjoy each other? Trust me. You don't need just one more corporate institutional happening in your life. Find a church where it feels like home and the people feel like family. If you don't feel that connection, don't make a judgment on the church. Bless them and recognize that you are simply discerning there is no grace to connect with this church.

Also, you may want to give the same church a few chances before jumping to conclusions.

Leadership

Evaluate the leadership of the church. Are the pastors and other leaders knowledgeable, approachable, and genuine in their faith?

Service Opportunities

Investigate to see if the church has opportunities for volunteering or serving the community. There are two ways to connect with a church:

1. Attend a small group

2. Serve. Most churches will have a way that just about anyone can serve. Find out where that place is and start there. Serve with excellence and faithfulness; don't worry about it being beneath you. If that is a worry, that's a red flag you should write down on a sticky note and discuss with someone sooner rather than later. Matthew 20:26 reminds us that we must first learn to be a servant to be great.

WHAT'S AT STAKE?

It is a question I always ask myself after completing a study: what is at stake if we choose not to integrate into a supernatural community? It is in the context of a community where we can find healing, restoration, and the discovery of dormant gifts, assignments, and possibilities.

I, too, have experienced hurt from the church, which caused me to walk away. Although I never doubted my belief in God, I did turn my back on His bride. During that time, I lacked significant fruit in my life. However, God pursued me, and in His mercy, He healed my broken heart and replaced it with a heart of flesh. Remarkably, He did it at the church where my heart was broken. While I do not encourage you to seek healing where you were hurt, I want you to know that God can use the church family to love you back to life. Once I was restored, the Lord unveiled one of my life's significant assignments.

I want this for every person, including you! What is at stake? A supernatural portal that you cannot find outside of the community. An opportunity for the adventure of a lifetime. I understand that people can be weird, inconsistent, and frustrating, but God loves all people, even with all their quirks. Your supernatural journey is a journey of trust and intimacy. Will you forgive those who have let you down? Will you forgive the church? Will you forgive yourself? Everything is at stake if you say no.

CHAPTER SIX

ACTIVATING THE MIRACLE REALM OF HEAVEN

"The healing power of God is available to everyone who believes. It doesn't matter who you are or what you've done, God's love and healing is for you."

—A.A. ALLEN

You will witness more miracles in the next twelve months than you have seen in the past twelve years, and these may not be limited to church settings. Through the power of God released from your hands, you will witness so many miracles that you might forget to celebrate them all. People will seek you out for prayers, ask you to visit them, call you on the phone, and even wait for you at your house. Once the news of your miracle-working abilities spreads, be prepared for an influx of people seeking your help.

In this chapter, I explain the number-one reason why most believers fail to see signs, wonders, and

miracles taking place through them. We will explore how believers often lose faith when faced with sickness and disease, and then I will provide you with tangible, practical, and actionable steps to help you start witnessing the release of captives.

NOT THE WAY IT WAS MEANT TO BE

If you turn on any cable news network, you will quickly see many issues, including wars, famine, corruption, poverty, and injustice. It only takes a moment to realize that humanity is grappling with the effects of thousands of years of generational iniquity and infirmity. The next time you see such headlines, say aloud, "This is not how it was meant to be." In the beginning, God created everything, and it was good. The Hebrew word for *good* is *towb,* which means "perfect in functional design and aesthetic beauty" (Strong's H2896). Everything was *towb!* But after the fall of man in Genesis 3, everything became fractured in beauty and design. Creation shifted from God's blessing to a curse, meaning it must survive at all costs.

Interestingly enough, Charles Darwin derived his theory of evolution from this observation, seeing how all created things had to fight for their survival. He believed that if forced to do so, creation would adapt, evolve, and fight to survive against natural conditions and predators, or it would become extinct. Darwin's initial observation was correct, but it could have been understood more thoroughly through the lens of Genesis 3.

With the fall and corruption of creation came an inherent expectation of death, and naturally, the fear of it followed.

This fear is seen through humanity's unwise choices. If people deny the existence of God and the idea of divine accountability, their selfishness and survival instinct will lead them into all manner of evil. The Bible refers to this as iniquity, defined as the internal bent within humanity to do wrong. Infirmity refers to both mental and physical weakness.

YOUR ACTIVATION BEGINS WITH HONESTY

The impact of generational iniquity and infirmity has affected all of us. Although we may want to focus on something other than the disappointing aspects of our lives, that is precisely where our journey to activating miracles must begin. Honesty is essential to gaining true empowerment in the area of the miraculous because sickness and disease affect everyone. People must possess the necessary tools to process their losses.

I want to ask you some questions, and I urge you to take a moment to answer them honestly. You may even want to record your responses in your journal. Suppose you have struggled with healing and miracles and have yet to experience this spiritual gift in your own life. In that case, these questions may provide valuable insight to help you overcome any obstacles hindering your progress. Please answer these questions with brutal honesty. It is a personal reflection between you and the Lord, and He can handle your uncensored brokenness.

1. How have sickness and disease impacted your life?

2. In what ways have sickness and disease affected your identity and self-image? Have you adopted any identity statements related to a disease,

such as "I am a diabetic" or "I am a cancer survivor"?

3. How has iniquity (sin) shaped your identity and self-image? Have you adopted any identity statements related to addiction, such as "I am an alcoholic" or "I am a sex addict"?

4. How has death and loss impacted your life?

5. How have death and loss impacted your belief in God?

6. Have you ever believed in healing and been disappointed? If so, how did that disappointment affect your belief in healing?

7. Have you ever prayed for someone's resurrection and been disappointed? If so, how did that disappointment affect your belief in God's character and nature as good and faithful?

8. How has suicide impacted your life? Did guilt and condemnation affect you?

9. In what ways are you still wrestling with any of the above factors?

TO THE BROKENHEARTED

If you are currently experiencing a season of painful loss and are struggling to understand where God fits in, take comfort in Psalm 51:17, as translated by Brian Simmons in The Passion Translation: "*The fountain of your pleasure is found in the sacrifice of my shattered heart before you. You will not despise my tenderness as I bow down humbly at your feet."*

This verse reveals God's character and willingness to draw near to brokenhearted people. It's common to feel lonely, abandoned, and vulnerable during pain, but remember that your pain is not offensive or intimidating to God. He longs to reveal His love and care for you in your brokenness.

When broken, you can either push people away or allow your tenderness to lead you into a vulnerability where you can heal and grow. The enemy will try to exploit your brokenness, but you can protect your soul against judgments by asking the Lord to help you keep your heart soft.

In 2 Corinthians 12:9-10, Paul reminds us that God's grace is sufficient for us, and His power is made perfect in our weakness. We don't need to have everything together when we come to Him. Our honesty about what we lack creates a supernatural magnet for His power.

To the brokenhearted, I encourage you to run to God with your open and broken heart. He promises that He will never reject or despise you for your brokenness. Remember that God's love for you is everlasting, and He promises to be with you in your pain.

If you're in a season of pain and loss, pray with me:

Heavenly Father, I come before You now, approaching You with boldness, humility, and a broken heart. I need You now more than ever. I need the kind of love and affection that can only come from a true and perfect Father. By faith, I declare Your powerful, tangible, and unwavering presence. I know I am not alone, and

You are always near me. I love You now and always. Amen.

THE NUMBER-ONE REASON WHY MOST BELIEVERS DO NOT SEE MIRACLES

You might think, *Wow, that was an intense way to begin a chapter on activating the miracle realm.* And you'd be right. Usually, when equipping people to walk in miracles, we build their faith by recalling numerous examples of healing. The idea is to create such a compelling case with powerful testimonies that the spirit of doubt will have no choice but to shrivel up and die.

However, doubt is only sometimes the root cause of why most people don't walk in miracles. While doubt is undoubtedly an issue, it's not necessarily the underlying problem. That's why we began the chapter the way we did. We need to address the effects and subconscious theology framed by lingering disappointment.

Imagine breaking your arm and not seeking medical attention to have the bone set and secured. The outcome will be that the bone will not heal correctly and the arm will eventually become permanently disfigured. Although the arm may heal, it won't heal as intended. It will lose its functionality and won't be able to perform its original purpose.

The same principle applies when we try to achieve emotional healing without the truth. We may move on from our past, but we will lose our supernatural ability to function in alignment with God's word. Instead, when faced with injustice, sin, sickness, or disease, we will position ourselves to avoid getting hurt again. We will adjust our theology in a way that allows us to merely survive.

Disappointment is often the root cause of why most believers don't experience miracles. When your soul isn't aligned with the truth of God's word, your mind, will, and emotions will heal distortedly, preventing you from functioning supernaturally.

The good news is that if you can humbly and honestly confront the disappointment and acknowledge how it has affected your faith, God can readily provide you with the grace and power to overcome it. Whether you were let down by a lack of healing or experienced loss due to a broken relationship, missed opportunity, or unfulfilled expectations, the enemy will always try to use disappointment to overwhelm you with feelings of discouragement, hurt, and uncertainty about the future.

Once you recognize that these emotions are just feelings and not rooted in truth, it's as though God turns on the light switch. We can shift these emotions by making light of them. My goal is to assist you in minimizing the impact of disappointment, so you can be strengthened by God's grace to reclaim your authority.

WAYS TO MAKE LIGHT OF DISAPPOINTMENT

Acknowledge your feelings when experiencing disappointment. It is essential to acknowledge your feelings and avoid suppressing them. Many people may try to ignore or deny their emotions, adopting a robotic and contrived demeanor as a religious response. However, in the shortest verse in the Bible in John 11:35, we're told Jesus wept. Jesus demonstrates that it is okay to feel and express grief. He wept over the loss of His friend Lazarus (even though minutes later, He would resurrect him from the dead), showing us that it is perfectly acceptable to grieve and acknowledge negative emotions.

The Bible encourages us to feel and express our emotions to the Lord. Psalm 62:8 (ESV) says, *"Trust in him at all times, O people; pour out your heart before him; God is a refuge for us."* Therefore, we can bring our disappointments to God in prayer and ask for comfort and strength.

Declaration for the Disappointed

> *As I grieve, I choose not to grieve like those without hope. I command my feelings, all of them, to come into alignment with the truth.*

Trust in God's Plan

Tragedy is never a part of our plans, and God is not the author of injustice. However, God can take what the enemy meant for evil and turn it around for His ultimate glory.

Proverbs 16:9 (NIV) states, *"In their hearts humans plan their course, but the Lord establishes their steps."* Even when things don't go according to our plans, we can trust that God is in control and has a purpose for our lives.

Romans 8:28 (NIV) assures us, saying, *"And we know that in all things God works for the good of those who love him, who have been called according to his purpose."* It means that no matter the tragedy, God's plan for our life cannot be thwarted unless we fail to trust Him. The degree to which tragedy affects God's plan for our life is solely determined by our ability or inability to trust Him.

Declaration for Your Destiny

This upset does not change God's plan for my life.

Refocus by Giving Thanks

When disappointment comes like a flood, letting the negatives consume our focus is easy. However, the Bible tells us that we can refocus by carving out a realm of thanksgiving by posturing our soul and framing gratitude over our attitude.

First Thessalonians 5:18 (NIV) says, *"give thanks in all circumstances; for this is God's will for you in Christ Jesus."* By focusing on the faithfulness of God and thanking God for His blessings, you can shift your perspective and find hope and joy amid disappointment.

Declaration of Thanksgiving

> *The peace of God, which surpasses all understanding, will guard my heart and mind in Christ Jesus (Philippians 4:7).*
>
> *I thank You, Lord, that this trial is not a punishment on me and that my punishment fell on Jesus. Instead, I see this trial as an opportunity for You to come as a faithful Father and reveal to me how close You are. Thank You for Your faithfulness and for being with me through this difficult time.*

God Is Not the Problem!

The first year of my pastoring journey was akin to a trial by fire. In just twelve months, I presided over eight funerals. I can still vividly recall like yesterday a moment when I was en route to visit a church member's house. The news had just broken that a mother of four had been diagnosed with fourth-stage cancer. As I drove, I mentally rehearsed how I would respond to her husband and kids—expressing my condolences, offering encouragement, and doing everything I could to comfort them.

That was the moment when anger began to stir within me. I couldn't help but question myself—what was I doing? This family had asked me to pray for their beloved mother and wife, hoping for her complete healing from cancer. Yet I found myself lacking faith in her recovery. In such situations, I felt like there was only one thing to do.

I yelled at God, "What's going on?" I said. "I know You are all-powerful, capable of healing this woman, but do I even believe You will?"

That's when it hit me—the irrationality of my anger. I wasn't upset with God but with myself. I realized I had no apparent belief regarding healing, and my lack of confidence in God's willingness to heal was the issue, not His ability.

I realized that I was the issue, and I didn't want to be the problem preventing someone from receiving their healing. I repented and declared, "God, I believe it is Your will to heal."

Something shifted inside me. I was already angry, but now I was mad at the right thing. I put the car in drive and got back on the road. When I arrived at the family's house, I came not as Pastor Darren with a rehearsed comfort agenda but as faith healer Darren with a plan to destroy the works of darkness. For the record, the woman did not experience a manifestation of healing, but God's grace was tremendously sufficient for the family. They are still part of my life today, and I have so much respect for the woman's husband, maturity, and service to the body of Christ. Her promotion from earth into Paradise didn't set me back.

I was on a new journey of trust and confidence in God. I immediately began listening to every teaching on healing I could find, starting with Bill Johnson's series called "Healing: Our Neglected Birthright" and Randy Clark's Healing School, which I highly recommend. Later on, I met Charlie Shamp, whom I had never met, someone who walked in such raw faith. His confidence in God was so strong that it was offensive. One of the greatest impartations I have ever received in faith has been from Charlie. My family and I have witnessed many miracles in the last 14 years of ministry. God is faithful, able, and willing.

If you struggle with the ministry of signs, wonders, and miracles, know God is not the problem. Once you recognize the real problem, you can step into the real solution.

God Is Willing

As I previously mentioned, the real issue in my example was not God's ability but rather my lack of confidence in His ability. In Matthew 8, a leper came to Jesus and said, "Lord, if You are willing, You can make me clean." Jesus responded, "I am willing; be clean." Immediately, the leper was healed.

This example is interesting because the leper's question reflected my doubts. I never questioned God's ability but rather His willingness to heal through me. I find Jesus' response inspiring, as He declares He is willing to help us. We should proclaim this truth over our lives, "He is able, *and* He is willing!"

Throughout my life, I have heard countless believers pray, "God, if it is Thy will, I ask that You would heal...." However, in the New Testament, Jesus never implies that He is unwilling to heal. He came to fulfill Isaiah 53:4 (NRSV), which states, "*Surely he has borne our infirmities and carried our diseases.*"

The reason why we may not see as many signs, wonders, and miracles today is not due to a lack of the Holy Spirit or a lack of revival. Instead, it is often due to our lack of practical trust in God. Once we identify the root of our unbelief, we can deconstruct it and build our faith on a foundation of God's faithfulness.

KNOW YOUR ENEMY

Ephesians 6:12 reminds us that our struggle is not against other humans but against the rulers, authorities, and spiritual forces of evil in the heavenly realms. This verse is part of a larger passage that discusses spiritual warfare and the importance of putting on the "full armor of God" to withstand the attacks of the devil, our true enemy.

When we face challenges like sin, sickness, and disease, we must remember that these are not battles against flesh but against the devil himself. Migraines, cancer, and chronic depression are all attacks from the enemy, as are temptations, lies, distractions, discouragement, and deception.

By recognizing the true source of our struggles, we can focus on fighting against the spiritual forces of evil rather than blaming other people. Unfortunately, many people do not experience the supernatural power of God in their prayers because they do not know how to pray effectively. It is often the result of a misdiagnosis of their spiritual battles.

Paul encourages us to prepare for spiritual warfare by putting on the whole armor of God, which includes truth, righteousness, faith, and the Word of God. Equipped with these tools, we can stand firm in our faith and resist all attacks from the devil.

YOU HAVE BEEN GIVEN AUTHORITY

Luke 9:1 states that Jesus gathered His twelve disciples and granted them the power and authority to cure diseases and cast out demons. It is important to note that this event occurred before Acts 2 and the baptism in the Holy Spirit. Jesus was not merely anointing or equipping His disciples but deputizing them. When deputized, they were appointed as a substitute, akin to a police deputy authorizing a civilian to make an arrest. The term *deputize* originally referred to when a deputy would delegate some of their authority to non-police officers, allowing them to act as a deputy when necessary.

Jesus recognized the presence of evil in the world and called on His disciples to confront the powers of darkness and bring healing and hope from the kingdom of heaven to those in need.

Just as the disciples were granted power and authority, so too have we been given the same ability to heal and cast out demons. Through unwavering faith, God works miracles in our lives and the lives of those around us. With His help, we can overcome obstacles and accomplish great things for His glorious kingdom.

A SAMPLE OF SUPERNATURAL AUTHORITY

I once dreamed of finding myself at the local mall food court. While there, I noticed a commotion outside in the parking lot. Curious, I went outside to investigate and saw two police officers trying to calm down a woman who seemed possessed by demons. She was growling and causing quite a disturbance. Despite the police officers' efforts, she remained uncontrollable, and at one point she even picked up one of their motorbikes and hurled it at one of the officers. I felt a strong urge to intervene, thinking someone needed to act.

Suddenly, I felt the power of God coursing through me, and I was filled with righteous anger. It felt like I was hulking up, with my muscles growing. I pointed my finger at the possessed woman and shouted one word: "You!" She looked up at me, and I woke up from the dream. Even after waking up, I still felt that same supernatural authority. It was as if the Lord had given me a taste of the supernatural authority I was about to possess.

SHALOM AND THE PURPOSE FOR THE SUPERNATURAL

We will explore the topic of healing and miracles as we build a systematic theology and philosophy for understanding the purpose of the supernatural. The current state of things is not how God intended it to be. However, we can observe instances of divine restoration when things are made right, giving us a glimpse of the world as it was meant to be—a reflection of the garden of the Lord before the effects of sin took hold. This moment of goodness and wholeness is what the Hebrews refer to as "shalom."

The concept of shalom encompasses the harmonious inter-weaving of God, humans, and all creation in equity, fulfillment, and delight. In the Bible, shalom signifies far more than mere peace of mind or a temporary cease-fire between enemies. It represents universal flourishing, wholeness, and delight—a state where natural needs are satisfied, and natural gifts are fruitfully employed under God's love. Shalom is what the world ought to be.

Anytime this state of flourishing and delight was disrupted, the ancients considered it a breach of justice. Shalom refers to the holistic wellbeing of the entire being, including the spirit, soul, and body. If one is healthy in both body and mind, they are experiencing shalom. But if one is suffering from psycho-logical or physical torment, this is seen as a loss of shalom and an act of injustice.

Considering this, when we witness Jesus healing the blind man by making mud with His saliva and spreading it on his eyes, we understand that this man has lost his physical shalom. God created the eyes to see; in this case, they could not perform their intended function. This loss of shalom is an act of injustice, and when Jesus heals the blind man, He is not suspending the natural order of things but restoring it. He is bringing shalom back, thereby executing justice.

In our culture, those celebrated for executing justice on behalf of the powerless are often referred to as *superheroes*.

SUPERHEROES

Superheroes significantly impact our culture, as they resonate with God's heart for humanity and the role of the righteous. It is evident the world celebrates superhero movies; they are among the highest-grossing movies in the entertainment industry.

For instance, *Avengers: Endgame* (2019) is currently the top-grossing movie of all time, earning over $2.79 billion worldwide. Several other superhero movies, such as *Avengers: Infinity War* (2018), *The Avengers* (2012), and *Black Panther* (2018) are among the top 20 highest-grossing movies of all time.[1]

"The joy of the righteous works justice, and ruin to evildoers" (Proverbs 21:15 ABPE). This word for "works" can also be translated as "executes." It is the role of the righteous to execute justice and restore shalom; it is our work and joy.

So how do we execute justice? Matthew 10:8 (ESV) states, *"Heal the sick, raise the dead, cleanse lepers, cast out demons. You received without paying; give without pay."* The ministry of signs, wonders, and miracles is the working of justice, which brings about shalom and human flourishing. It opens a window to glimpse how things used to be in Eden and reveal the future restoration of all things when King Jesus returns.

What does it look like to have a generation of unapologetically supernatural believers? It is a modern-day, real-life justice league, those who fear no evil and have a revelation of their authority in Christ, using their lives to displace all the works of the evil one.

THE VILLAINS

Now that we have determined that you are an unapologetically supernatural superhero called to execute justice and reestablish shalom, we must see that every superhero has villains. In this hour, the supernatural church faces three significant foes: apathy, Gnosticism, and materialism.

1. Apathy

Apathy is a formidable foe for the supernatural Christian, and its dangers are not underestimated. Apathy is a master of deception, lulling believers into a false sense of security with its lack of interest, enthusiasm, and concern. It is a force that seeks to destroy faith and rob you of your passion for God.

One of the apathy's most insidious weapons is its ability to stunt spiritual growth. By encouraging complacency and a lack of effort, apathy will aim to prevent you from developing a deeper relationship with God. Its goal is to keep you stagnant, spiritually lazy, disconnected, and uninterested, preventing you from reaching your full potential.

Apathy also encourages neglect of responsibilities. As the villain, it wants nothing more than to convince you that you are powerless and unable to offer hope to the hopeless. It knows that by causing you to neglect your assignments, it can cause harm to both you and those around you.

Furthermore, apathy is a master of temptation attempting to lead you down a path of sin and spiritual decay. It will try to make you indifferent to sin, lowering your guard against temptation and making you vulnerable to its attacks. Its goal is to destroy your faith and cause you to fall away from God.

Finally, apathy will seek to hinder your ability to fulfill God's purpose for your life. Becoming apathetic will prevent you from seeing and seizing divine opportunities to see God show up and show off in your life. Its ultimate goal is to prevent you from fulfilling your destiny.

2. Gnosticism

Gnosticism is an ancient belief system that promotes the idea that salvation can be attained through secret knowledge rather than faith in the Savior. It's a dangerous belief system that can lead you astray from the true message of the gospel, which is that our salvation comes by grace through faith in Jesus Christ alone.

As a superhero, you have a great responsibility to uphold the values of justice, compassion, and humility. But Gnosticism would lead you down a path of pride, elitism, exclusivity, and neglect of the world that Jesus died to save. Gnosticism is a villain that seeks to distort the truth and mislead you through a plethora of mystical widgets, formulas, and add-ons. Gnosticism comes to overcomplicate everything, making salvation, healing, deliverance, and inner healing so tricky that only paid professionals should do it.

Jesus said it best in Matthew 18:3 (ESV) when He said, *"Truly, I say to you, unless you turn and become like children, you will never enter the kingdom of heaven."* Listen, if a third grader can't understand your theology, you may be in danger of coming under the influence of Gnosticism.

So please, be cautious and vigilant against this villain. Stay grounded in the central and straightforward message of the supernatural gospel of Jesus Christ and remain faithful to your calling as a superhero. Remember, your most excellent power lies not in secret knowledge but in your unwavering faith in the Savior and your commitment to restoring shalom for all.

3. Busyness

In today's fast-paced world, busyness has become a status symbol, but it can also be a trap that distracts you from your true calling. You will miss opportunities to be unapologetically supernatural when you are too busy.

This is one of the big villains we attack at Portals University, a mentorship program that helps people identify, steward, and maximize divine opportunities from heaven. Please be careful and discerning in managing your time. Remember that people compromise their call and assignments daily because they are constantly too busy and overwhelmed. Our obedience to the Lord is contingent on our ability to prioritize our time and commitments wisely, making time for rest, reflection, and self-care.

Be aware of the danger of the villain of busyness, and stay faithful to your calling. Your most extraordinary power comes not from being constantly busy but from being present and attentive to the voice of the Lord, the needs of others, and the leading of the Holy Spirit.

CONFRONTING SICKNESS AND DISEASE

Since we are discussing superheroes and villains, it's worth noting that there are no new villains. Therefore, we can learn a lot from previous superheroes from previous generations who successfully defeated them. One such hero was American evangelist, revivalist, and faith healer A.A. Allen, who uniquely tackled sickness and disease. Allen believed sickness and disease were caused by demonic possession or oppression and could be cast out through faith and prayer.

His healing ministry became one of the largest and most significant in the United States during the 1950s and 1960s. He witnessed numerous miraculous healings, including cancer, blindness, and paralysis. His approach to healing through deliverance significantly influenced how we heal the sick today. Allen found his greatest inspiration in Jesus, who also approached infirmity as foreign to God's perfect plan and demonic. As we see in the healing ministry of Christ, Allen followed a similar path to giving sickness and disease a heavenly beatdown!

Luke 4:38-41 (NIV) says:

> *Jesus left the synagogue and went to the home of Simon. Now Simon's mother-in-law was suffering from a high fever, and they asked Jesus to help her. So he bent over her and rebuked the fever, and it left her. She got up at once and began to wait on them. At sunset, the people brought to Jesus all who had various kinds of sickness, and laying his hands on each one, he healed them. Moreover, demons came out of many people, shouting, "You are the Son of God!" But he rebuked them and would not allow them to speak, because they knew he was the Messiah.*

Another example can be found in Matthew 8:16-17 (NIV):

> *When evening came, many who were demon-possessed were brought to him, and he drove out the spirits with a word and healed all the sick. This was*

to fulfill what was spoken through the prophet Isaiah:
"He took up our infirmities and bore our diseases."

We can follow in the footsteps of Jesus and A.A. Allen by confronting sickness and disease as they did, by rebuking it as a demon and an impostor and recognizing it as not a part of God's perfect plan. As we learn to stand in Christ's authority, our boldness will grow, and we can cast out demons and witness countless miracles and healings.

HOW TO HEAL THE SICK

There are multiple ways to heal the sick, as Jesus demonstrated throughout His ministry. He used various methods such as laying hands on the person, speaking a word of healing, or simply willing the person to be healed. Additionally, He employed physical elements such as mud, spit, or oil in some cases. The book of Acts recounts how people would lay their sick on the streets so when Peter passed by, his shadow might fall on them and heal them. Similarly, handkerchiefs and aprons that Paul had touched were used to heal the sick and drive out evil spirits.

Quick and fun story for you on this topic. I once had the honor of training young people in supernatural evangelism. While in a neighborhood, we approached an older woman and shared the message of Jesus with her. After gaining permission to bless her, I asked her to stand where my shadow was. I gave thanks to the Lord, and she reported that she could feel something. She began to freak out, declaring, "I have goosebumps all over my body!" When I inquired about her experience, she confirmed that she felt the presence of God. I explained the significance of her encounter, and she received Jesus as her Lord and Savior.

We often need clarification on the methodology or the tools, and this is where we can become vulnerable to the pitfalls of Gnosticism. It's important to note that my shadow or Paul's handkerchiefs hold no magical power. Instead, the power of God is activated through simple childlike obedience and humble faith in the believer. The lady in my shadow exhibited such humble faith, so God honored her with a powerful encounter.

GETTING STARTED

Healing someone can feel like trying to lift a bus on your own. It's impossible without God's help. That's why it's important not to rely solely on your strength. Charisma and style may impress people but won't bring true healing. Only the presence of the Lord can do that.

To start, invite the presence of the Lord. It isn't about trying to summon God from heaven to earth—He's already here. It's about partnering with Him and acknowledging His power. Take your time with this. Don't rush. Begin by welcoming the Holy Spirit like an old friend. Enjoy His company and soak up His presence.

When praying for someone's healing, imagine them as an empty cup. Now, invite the Holy Spirit into the scene, picturing His presence as a powerful waterfall. Visualize the waterfall filling the cup, overflowing it, and cleaning it. Welcome the Holy Spirit to increase in intensity, "More, Holy Spirit. Come!" Next, picture the Holy Spirit as a waterfall of fire, reminiscent of the pillars of fire that appeared to the 120 in the upper room. Welcome the fire of God to enter the person and command everything not of the Holy Spirit to reveal itself. And it will!

Take your time and patiently use your authority to command every spirit that is not of the Holy Spirit to leave and go to the pit in the name of Jesus. Be patient. Use your authority. And watch as King Jesus lifts the bus off the ground for you.

Remember to have fun and be obedient to the still, small voice of the Holy Spirit. Pastor Surprise in Nelspruit, South Africa, who has raised numerous people from the dead, once said that every resurrection he has ever seen was a matter of simple obedience to the Lord. Don't get addicted to a method; instead, be addicted to His presence and obedient to His voice, and He will do the impossible through you.

HEALING THROUGH THE LAYING ON OF HANDS

While it is true that healing can manifest in the glory realm without physical touch, it's worth noting that laying on hands was a prevalent method of healing throughout the New Testament. The book of Acts, for instance, repeatedly mentions the apostles laying hands on the sick for healing (see Acts 8:17; 19:6). In my ministry, I have found this to be the most common way people experience healing.

During my interview with NPR amidst the coronavirus pandemic, the reporter brought up a point, saying, "In my research about your church, I noticed that you guys like to touch people."

I responded, "I wouldn't phrase it quite like that."

It appeared she was intentionally trying to provoke a reaction from me, as reporters often do. She argued that she found it surprising how physically affectionate we were, especially when our governor had mandated social distancing to prevent the spread of illness, requiring people to stay at least six feet apart.

I informed her that the practice of laying on of hands is a time-honored tradition that spans back thousands of years and was practiced by both Jesus and His disciples. This act involves physically touching or laying hands on someone to impart blessings, healing, and release the power of God. I emphasized that physical touch is not just a command to the church to activate the supernatural but also a powerful way to express and communicate love.

I shared with her some of the alarming teenage suicide statistics that peaked during the pandemic, statistics that reached unprecedented levels due to inappropriate government-ordered isolation mandates and the stress created by the media's unending fear-mongering. I explained that the depression and stress caused by the government's COVID-19 isolation strategies were the real killers and that by being obedient to God's word, Christians would save more lives than the vaccine ever could.

UPGRADES ARE POSSIBLE!

Lastly, let me note that upgrades are possible. Anointings can be transferred and imparted. Many things in the kingdom of God can be taught, but some must be caught or imparted.

Prophetess Stacey Campbell has an interesting story about how early on in her ministry, she would never see healings and miracles. Finally, she received impartation prayer, and the healing realm opened. I've heard many stories like this over the years. You trace the healing generals from the early 1900s into the 1980s. They are almost all connected through the laying on of hands. The anointing for healing is transferable.

Impartation prayer is simply the Holy Spirit's anointing, and power is transmitted from one person to another through the laying on of hands. Spiritual gifts, such as prophecy, healing, and speaking in tongues, can be transferred and imparted through the laying on of hands.

> *For this reason I remind you to fan into flame the gift of God, which is in you through the laying on of my hands. For the Spirit God gave us does not make us timid, but gives us power, love and self-discipline. So do not be ashamed of the testimony about our Lord or of me his prisoner. Rather, join with me in suffering for the gospel, by the power of God* (2 Timothy 1:6-8 NIV).

ACTIVATION PRAYER

I am a radical fanatical believer!

I believe that not only does God still heal the sick, but that I am a faith healer, a dead raiser, a holy exorcist, empowered by the Holy Spirit to execute justice, drive out darkness, and see the peace of God restored. I will see the eyes of the blind opened. I will see the mute sing for joy. I will see the lame leap like a dear.

I will see the dead awaken. The glory of the Lord in my life will not fade away. This glory will increase from glory to glory. I will never apologize for practicing His presence. I was created to be unapologetically supernatural. This is who I am. I am not sorry. For I am His! Amen.

NOTE

1. Reuters, "Top 10 Highest-Grossing Movies," July 21, 2019. https://www.reuters.com/graphics/USA-FILM -AVENGERS/0100B09V0ME/index.html.

CHAPTER SEVEN

THE NIGHT IS FOR THE SUPERNATURAL— YOUR DREAM MANUAL

"The night is a time of profound reflection when we can connect with the spiritual world and seek guidance from God."
—THOMAS MERTON, *The Positive Aspects of the Night*

God created night—it was His idea, and this incredible creation holds great significance and opportunity for the sons and daughters of God. The beauty of the night sky, the stars, and the moon are humbling and awe-inspiring, and they constantly remind us of the existence, greatness, and power of our mighty God!

And God said, "Let there be light," and there was light. And God saw that the light was good. And God separated the light from the darkness. God called the

155

light Day, and the darkness he called Night. And there was evening and there was morning, the first day (Genesis 1:3-5 ESV).

God created the stars and the moon on the fourth day of creation, as described in Genesis 1:14 (ESV), "*And God said, 'Let there be lights in the expanse of the heavens to separate the day from the night. And let them be for signs and for seasons, and for days and years.'*"

At night, these stars and the moon serve as a source of light in the darkness. Before the invention of artificial lighting, the stars and the moon provided the only light source at night. It would have been particularly important for the ancients, allowing them to navigate and perform various tasks. The stars and the moon served as a way to measure time. The phases of the moon were used to create the lunar calendar, which is still used in some parts of the world. The stars were also used to navigate the oceans and determine the seasons. If you were a traveler and lost your way, you would wait for the night so heaven's road map could unfold.

David has his take on the moon and stars; they were motivations of awe-inspiring praise and worship to the Lord. In the Aramaic Bible in Plain English translation of Psalm 136:9, David proclaims, "*The moon and the stars for rulers of the night, for his mercies are to eternity.*" Just like the stars and the moon continue, night after night, from generation to generation, the mercies of God continue to endure into eternity.

Throughout the word of God, the night is often symbolic of prayer, rest, and reflection. In Psalm 63:6 (GW), David says, "*As I lie on my bed, I remember you. Through the long hours of the night, I think about you."* The night is a time of peace and quiet when we can focus on our relationship with God and draw closer to Him.

THE NEGATIVE ASPECTS OF THE NIGHT

However, for many people, maybe most, the night doesn't seem like something created by God. One of my children once told me that God created the day, but Satan created the night. When I corrected her, she informed me that this wasn't her idea but rather one of her friends. Since then, my daughter has made new friends.

Her concept of the night as being associated with darkness and evil is not uncommon. For many, the night serves as a reminder of the darkness in the world, both literally and supernaturally. It is also reflected in the word of God. John 3:19-20 (NIV) says, *"This is the verdict: Light has come into the world, but people loved darkness instead of light because their deeds were evil. Everyone who does evil hates the light, and will not come into the light for fear that their deeds will be exposed."* The night is often associated with darkness, which is used as a symbol of evil and sin, a time when people think they can get away with deeds that could not be committed during the day.

As Psalm 91:5-6 (NIV) indicates, *"You will not fear the terror of night, nor the arrow that flies by day, nor the pestilence that stalks in the darkness, nor the plague that destroys at midday."* This text refers to the kind of danger associated with the night. Before the invention of electricity, the night was a dangerous time, especially for travelers and vulnerable populations.

Zephaniah 1:12 (NIV) associates the night with judgment or punishment: "*At that time I will search Jerusalem with lamps and punish those who are complacent, who are like wine left on its dregs, who think, 'The Lord will do nothing, either good or bad.'*"

The night is also associated with spiritual warfare, as darkness is often used as a symbol of the devil and his influence. Ephesians 6:12 (ESV) declares, "*For we do not wrestle against flesh and blood, but against the rulers, against the authorities, against the cosmic powers over this present darkness, against the spiritual forces of evil in the heavenly places.*"

YOU NEED THE NIGHT

Sleep is a fundamental physiological process essential for our health and wellbeing. In recent years, scientific research has made great strides in understanding the mechanisms underlying sleep and its impact on physical and mental health. As believers, we must constantly be reminded (because we are constantly forgetting) that our bodies are temples of the Holy Spirit and that taking care of our physical health is a part of the stewardship that He requires of us.

The Bible clearly states that we need the night. Psalm 127:2 (NIV) says, "*In vain you rise early and stay up late, toiling for food to eat—for he grants sleep to those he loves.*" The need for rest is part of God's design for us, and He has created and gifted us with rest and rejuvenation as an essential component of that process.

Recent scientific findings have highlighted the critical role that sleep plays in our physical and mental health.

For example, sleep is crucial for memory consolidation, allowing our brains to process and integrate information learned during waking hours. It leads to improved memory recall and performance.

Deep sleep, also known as slow-wave sleep, is particularly important for physical recovery, immune function, and cognitive processes such as memory and learning. During this sleep stage, the body produces cytokines, a type of protein that helps fight off infection and inflammation.

Chronic sleep deprivation has been linked to various metabolic disorders, including obesity, insulin resistance, and diabetes. Lack of sleep has also been shown to suppress immune function and increase the risk of infections. As believers, we are called to care for our bodies and prioritize rest and rejuvenation to promote physical health and prevent illness.

We even see a connection between rest and mental health in Matthew 11:28-30 (NIV) when Jesus says, *"Come to me, all you who are weary and burdened, and I will give you rest. Take my yoke upon you and learn from me, for I am gentle and humble in heart, and you will find rest for your souls. For my yoke is easy and my burden is light."*

As you understand that the night was created for God's supernatural sons and daughters, you will reframe the night and take authority over areas where you have felt powerless. This chapter can potentially be one of the most transformative sections in this book, impacting your life in significant ways. By engaging with the different scriptures, processes, activations, and declarations, you can experience transformation through your mind's renewal. When you realize that the night is intended for the supernatural, you will bid farewell to the anxiety and stress that have previously framed the nighttime.

AMERICANS ARE NOT SLEEPING

In today's fast-paced society, it seems like everyone is constantly on the go, working long hours and trying to fit as much as possible into their already busy schedules. As a result, many Americans are sacrificing their sleep to keep up with the demands of their daily lives. This chronic sleep deprivation is having a significant impact on our health and wellbeing.

Research has shown that adults need an average of seven to nine hours of sleep per night to function at their best, but many Americans are getting far less than that. According to the Centers for Disease Control and Prevention, more than one-third of American adults report getting less than the recommended amount of sleep regularly.

The effects of sleep deprivation are widespread and can impact every aspect of a person's life. Lack of sleep can impair cognitive function, making it more difficult to concentrate, solve problems, and make decisions. It can also affect mood, leading to increased irritability, anxiety, and depression. Yes, there is a well-established link between sleep deprivation and depression. In fact, sleep disturbance is one of the diagnostic criteria for major depressive disorder in the Diagnostic and Statistical Manual of Mental Disorders (DSM-5).

Research has shown that sleep deprivation can rewire the brain leading to chronic depression. For example, a lack of sleep can alter the prefrontal cortex, which regulates mood and emotion. Sleep deprivation also disrupts the balance of neurotransmitters in the brain, such as serotonin and dopamine, which helps us regulate our mood.

Furthermore, the relationship between sleep and depression is bidirectional, meaning that sleep deprivation can contribute to the development of depression, but depression can also cause sleep deprivation. Many individuals with depression experience insomnia or hypersomnia, worsening their symptoms and contributing to a cycle of negative mood and poor sleep.

New evidence also shows that treating sleep deprivation can be an effective way to improve symptoms of depression. Some studies have found that treating insomnia in individuals with depression can significantly improve their mood and overall functioning. Sleep deprivation has been linked to obesity, diabetes, cardiovascular disease, and other chronic health conditions.

Perhaps most concerning is the impact of sleep deprivation on safety. Drowsy driving is a major cause of car accidents, with the National Highway Traffic Safety Administration estimating that up to 6,000 fatal crashes each year are caused by drowsy driving.

Supernatural Vulnerability

For centuries, people have always been intrigued by the idea that the veil between our world and the world of the supernatural is thinner at night. Many cultures have their legends and beliefs about supernatural vulnerability at night, suggesting that we are more susceptible to encounters with these supernatural entities and realms when the sun goes down.

Evening heavenly visitations and prophetic dreams are significant themes throughout the Bible. These events often serve as a means of communication from God to His people, offering guidance, comfort, and warning. One of my favorite evening supernatural encounters is Abraham's encounter with God in Genesis 15. In this encounter, God comes to Abraham, appears to him in a vision, and promises him a great reward. Abram, still called by his original name before God changes it to Abraham in Genesis 17, responds by expressing his doubts about having an heir since he and his wife Sarai are childless. God then makes a covenant with Abram, promising him his descendants will be as numerous as the stars in the sky. The covenant is symbolized by a ritual in which Abram sacrifices animals and God passes between the pieces of the animals, indicating that He is making a solemn vow to fulfill His promise to Abram.

Another of my favorite evening encounters is the story of Jacob's ladder in Genesis 28:10-22. In this story, Jacob has a dream in which he sees a ladder stretching from earth to heaven, with angels ascending and descending on it. God speaks to Jacob in the dream, promising to bless him and his descendants.

In Genesis 37, God gives Joseph two prophetic dreams in which he sees his brothers bowing down to him. His brothers are not exactly fans of these dreams, and his brothers end up selling him into slavery in Egypt, but this unfortunate event serves as the catalyzing footstep by which Joseph eventually rises to power in Egypt.

Here's another aspect of supernatural vulnerability to which you can relate. During sleep, our soul doesn't necessarily operate within conscious boundaries like when awake.

The self-censoring mechanisms we use to manage and process the data we experience throughout our lives turns off, and our brain works to replay, reconcile, and integrate past experiences.

When we enter REM sleep, the stage in which we start to dream, our brain becomes highly active, our muscles become paralyzed, and our breathing and heart rate become irregular. Typically, we experience three to five REM sleep cycles per night, and if we get an average of seven to eight hours of sleep, we could be dreaming for up to ninety minutes each night!

During all this brain activity, the body enters a deep state of rest and recovery, making REM sleep a crucial sleep stage. Although we lose consciousness during sleep, our spirit remains awake and aware. Our spirit can communicate and replay information to our subconscious and conscious mind and even wake us up if necessary.

SPIRIT MAN ALARM SYSTEM

Andrea and I had been looking forward to our weekend in Seattle for weeks. We had planned everything meticulously, from the places to visit, to the restaurants where we would dine. Our hotel, an old building converted into a chic, boutique hotel for hipsters, was the perfect place to stay.

As we settled in for the night, I sensed something was off. There was an eerie feeling in the air, and I couldn't shake the feeling that we weren't alone in the room. Hours later, I was awakened when something hit the lamp next to me, and I sensed a spiritual presence in the room. Although I didn't say anything out loud, I felt my spirit man come up and to the front of my body, rebuking a demon that was present.

To my surprise, a bright explosion of light filled the room, and I could see the demon as a large, slimy, octopus-like creature with tentacles that filled the space. One of the tentacles was reaching straight out, inches away from my face. After the explosion cleared, the room went dark and quiet, and the spirit disappeared.

Years later, I shared this experience with a seer prophet who told me that he often saw this type of being in hotels. He explained that it was a spirit of lust and advised believers to be sure to clean their hotel rooms with the blood of Jesus before staying in them. I shared this information with Andrea, who had also sensed that something was wrong with our room spiritually, and she thanked me for telling her.

Get Ready — Night Is Coming

Unsurprisingly, many people struggle with getting a good night's sleep. Unfortunately, the topic of sleep is not typically covered in school or church, including how to prepare for sleep, how to steward our dreams, and how to be ready for what the Lord wants to reveal to us during the night. However, as we spend a third of our lives in bed, we should view our sleep as an opportunity for supernatural downloads and divine equipping to advance the kingdom of God the next day.

Rather than feeling like victims of the night, we should proactively prepare ourselves for it and take control of our bodies, dreams, and ability to sleep. Doing so can teach important life lessons, such as walking in our authority and stewarding the supernatural. It is important to recognize that sleep is essential in preparing our spirit, body, and soul for living a supernatural life during the day. Therefore, we should prioritize preparing for the night during the day, knowing that our sleep can profoundly impact our ability to progress and advance in our lives.

SHUTTING DOWN THE DREAM REALM

As a child, my fear of the dark and the nightmares that plagued me every night made it difficult to fall asleep. I would lie awake in bed, dreading the moment when my mind would inevitably transport me to a terrifying alternate reality. The dreams were so vivid and realistic that I often had trouble distinguishing them from reality.

My parents tried to help me by teaching me about the power of prayer and how to rebuke evil spirits in the name of Jesus. I was also equipped by the music of contemporary Christian songwriter Carman, who excellently modeled how to take authority over darkness.

However, one particular dream shook me to my core. In the dream, I found myself face to face with a demon. I followed my parents' advice and tried to rebuke the spirit in the name of Jesus, but to my horror, the demon laughed and told me that my efforts would not work this time. I was paralyzed with fear but kept repeating the words "in the name of Jesus" until I woke up, sweating and panting.

After that experience, I was even more terrified of going to sleep. I knew I needed to do something to regain control of my dreams and mind. That's when I came up with the idea of crafting a prayer I could say every night before bed. I wanted to make sure that my mind was protected from any dark or scary dreams, so I would pray every night the same prayer: "Dear Jesus, help me to have no dreams. Not even one!"

To my amazement, the prayer worked. I would fall asleep and wake up feeling rested and refreshed, without memory of any dreams. Even though I knew I was still dreaming on some level, the prayer gave me a sense of control and security, allowing me to sleep peacefully for many years.

Here's Why the Prayer Worked!

Our words have the power to open and close realms of the spirit. However, many believers are not aware of the impact of their words and often speak without understanding the consequences. We can see significant changes in our lives when we approach the Lord with intention and consistency. Daily prayer has the power to shift things in our lives, and it's essential to ask the Lord for what we need. Do you have a consistent daily prayer practice? What are you asking the Lord for?

Opening the Dream Realm Back Up!

Andrea and I discussed dreams during dinner with Bobby Conner and Paul Keith Davis. When Paul Keith asked me if I dream, I replied that I used to but had shut down that realm. He encouraged me to reopen it, and so, through consistent nightly prayer, the realm opened back up as easily as I closed it.

Now, when I put my children to bed, I pray a hybrid version of this prayer with them: "Dear Jesus, give my children good dreams. Dreams of heaven, dreams of angels, and dreams of You." It's short and sweet, but it works. By God's grace, my kids have had vivid encounters with angels while conscious and in the dream realm. We haven't had to deal with too many demons or nightmares.

DEALING WITH NIGHTTIME DEFEATER BELIEFS

As humans, we all struggle with lies we mistakenly believe are true. These lies are often called "defeater beliefs" because they can hinder us and prevent us from living according to God's will for our lives.

Defeater beliefs are typically rooted in fear, shame, or other negative emotions. They may be beliefs we have internalized from childhood, or they may be beliefs we have developed due to negative experiences or trauma. When we believe these lies, we give them power over our lives and allow them to defeat us. We may feel stuck, hopeless, or unworthy, and we may struggle to live in accordance with God's will for our lives.

Defeater beliefs can significantly impact our sleep, as they can create anxiety and stress that make it difficult to fall asleep or stay asleep throughout the night. When we believe lies contradicting God's word, we may experience negative emotions like fear, shame, or guilt, disrupting our sleep and leaving us tired and drained.

Examples of sleep-defeater beliefs may include:

1. "I'll never be able to fall asleep."

2. "If I don't get enough sleep, I won't be able to function."

3. "I'm too stressed to sleep."

4. "I'll never be able to overcome my insomnia."

5. "I have too much on my mind to sleep."

6. "I'll never be able to catch up on my sleep."

These beliefs can create a vicious cycle of anxiety and sleeplessness, as worrying about not getting enough sleep can make it even harder to fall asleep. A lack of sleep can make us even more susceptible to proclaiming and believing these lies.

To overcome these limiting beliefs, it is essential to recognize them as lies and replace them with the truth. Take time to reflect on the "facts" you hold about your experiences at night. These may be negative thoughts or emotions you have internalized, such as fear or anxiety, and prevent you from experiencing restful sleep. Identify as many of these beliefs as possible and write them down in your journal.

Once you have identified these beliefs, ask Jesus to reveal the truth about these situations. Cross out each negative belief and replace it with the truth that Jesus has shown you. Use scripture verses to support this truth and record them in your journal as a reminder of the power of God's word.

It can be challenging to identify and overcome these beliefs on our own, so seeking support from a pastor, counselor, or ministry such as Restoring the Foundations or SOZO can be incredibly helpful in this process. They can provide guidance and help to disrupt these defeater beliefs, allowing you to experience greater freedom and rest in your life.

PRAYER

Each night before you go to bed, take out your journal and pray:

Jesus, forgive me for believing and empowering the lie that_____, and I confess the truth that _____.
I declare this scripture over my night: _____ _____. Amen!

By embracing the truth, we can overcome our defeater beliefs and live in the freedom and power of a transformed mind.

DECLARATION

As a child of God, I believe that sleep is a precious gift from my Father. Therefore, I declare I will enjoy a peaceful and restful night's sleep tonight. I trust His goodness to grace me the rest needed to advance His kingdom tomorrow.

Practical Ways to Get Ready to Sleep!

There are some practical ways to prepare for sleep that will not include counting sheep, tossing and turning, and scrolling through social media all night long. First things first, start by carving out a pre-sleep routine. No, I'm not talking about a full spa treatment but rather simple activities that signal to your brain that it's time to begin preparing for the most important time of the day—nighttime. Maybe it's reading the Bible, preferably a non-digital copy, taking a warm bath, or soaking with your favorite instrumental worship album. The idea is to have a time of the night when stimulation and stress are not allowed.

Here are some practical ways to prepare for sleep and get the best night's rest possible:

1. Stick to a consistent sleep schedule: Try to go to bed and wake up at the same time every day, even on weekends.

2. Create a sleep-conducive environment: Ensure your bedroom is cool, quiet, and dark. Use blackout curtains, earplugs, or a white noise machine if necessary.

3. Avoid caffeine, alcohol, and nicotine: These substances can interfere with sleep. Try to avoid consuming them for several hours before bedtime.

4. Limit screen time: The blue light emitted by electronic devices can interfere with your body's natural sleep-wake cycle. Try to avoid using electronic devices for at least an hour before bed.

5. Exercise regularly: Regular exercise can help improve sleep quality, but avoid exercising too close to bedtime, as it can be stimulating.

6. Avoid large meals and beverages before bedtime: Eating a large meal or drinking a lot of fluids within three hours of bedtime can cause discomfort and disrupt sleep.

7. Invest in a new and better mattress and

pillows: A comfortable bed can significantly affect how well you sleep.

8. Manage stress: High stress levels can make falling asleep and staying asleep difficult.

9. Once asleep, begin dreaming as quickly as possible.

CONCERNING DREAMING

Supernatural dreams have been an awe-inspiring part of God's communication with humanity throughout the ages and featured prominently in the Bible from the Old Testament to the New Testament. They have been used as a powerful tool by God to reveal His plans, share His wisdom, and impart His supernatural gifts to those who seek Him.

Dreams from God should be a natural and exciting part of our supernatural journey. Each dream has the potential to bring us closer to God and reveal new insights about ourselves and our relationship with Him. When we learn to honor the night and our sleep and value the Lord's guidance through dreams, we begin to carve out a realm to the limitless possibilities of who God is.

The apostle Peter quotes the prophet Joel in Acts 2:17 (NIV), saying, "*In the last days, God says, I will pour out my Spirit on all people. Your sons and daughters will prophesy, your young men will see visions, your old men will dream dreams.*" You are enabled by the infilling of the Holy Spirit to have supernatural dreams and visions!

SEVEN TYPES OF BIBLICAL DREAMS

1. Prophetic Dreams

Prophetic dreams reveal insights and details into events. They can also forecast future events. Examples include Joseph's dreams in Genesis 37, in which he dreams that he will rule over his brothers, and Pharaoh's dreams in Genesis 41, in which he dreams of seven fat cows eaten by seven lean cows.

2. Symbolic Dreams

These are dreams that use symbols to convey a message. For example, in Daniel 2, Nebuchadnezzar dreams of a statue made of different materials, which Daniel interprets as representing different kingdoms.

3. Warning Dreams

These are dreams that warn of impending danger or judgment. For example, in Matthew 2, Joseph has a dream warning him to flee to Egypt with Mary and Jesus to escape Herod's wrath.

4. Instructional Dreams

These are dreams that provide guidance or instruction. For example, in Genesis 28, Jacob has a dream in which he sees a ladder stretching from earth to heaven and hears God's voice instructing him to carry on his journey.

5. Healing Dreams

These are dreams that provide healing or restoration. For example, in Genesis 20, God warns Abimelech in a dream to return Sarah to Abraham, which leads to his household's healing from infertility.

6. Spiritual Warfare

Dreams are also used in the Bible to depict spiritual warfare between good and evil forces. For example, the book of Revelation contains many dreamlike visions of the battle between God and Satan.

7. Visions

Although not strictly dreams, visions are similar and are also mentioned in the Bible. These are supernatural experiences in which God reveals something to the viewer. Visions like augmented reality are supernatural movies playing on top of your vision. For example, in Acts 9, Saul has a vision of Jesus on the road to Damascus, which leads to his conversion.

HOW TO DREAM DREAMS!

So as we have already stated, don't just haphazardly go to bed. Take some time to frame the night. As we have shown, you can do this through crafted prayers, but there are additional ways that you can intentionally go into the most important time of the day.

1. Expectation

Hebrews 11:6 says that without faith, it's impossible to please God. Before going to bed, activate your faith and set high expectations. Believe that you will receive God's guidance, direction, inspiration, and wisdom.

2. Clear the Clutter

Colossians 3:2 says to set your mind on things that are above, not on things that are on earth. Before going to sleep, take an inventory of your worries and take captive all vain, unproductive, and unfruitful thoughts (see 2 Corinthians 10:5). Clear the clutter of your mind before you even turn out the light. Remember Philippians 4:8 (ESV):

> *Finally, brothers, whatever is true, whatever is honorable, whatever is just, whatever is pure, whatever is lovely, whatever is commendable, if there is any excellence, if there is anything worthy of praise, think about these things.*

3. Get Your Dream Journal Ready

Keep a dream journal by your bedside and write down any dreams or impressions that come to you at night. More on this to come later in this chapter.

4. Submit the Night to the Lord

If you are concerned about demonic dreams or manifestations, declare the blood of Jesus over your room, your body, mind, and spirit. Declare Isaiah 54:17, "No weapon formed against me shall prosper!" Give thanks to the Lord for His protection and the amazing rest, peace, dreams, visions, and revelation you will receive during the night.

Example Prayer

> *King Jesus, thank You for tonight! Even as I sleep, my spirit will commune in union with Your Spirit. I will awaken tomorrow morning with guidance, inspiration, and wisdom. I thank You for the dreams from Your heart tonight. You are my refuge place and shield, and I thank You that You will keep me far from all unfruitful and unholy thoughts, dreams, and spirits. I trust that You will provide me with the clarity and insight I need to move forward and help advance Your kingdom on earth. Thank You for Your love, mercy, and grace. Amen!*

HOW TO REMEMBER YOUR DREAMS!

Some people say to me that they don't dream. The science says otherwise. It's not a matter of whether you dream or not but whether or not you remember your dreams. Some say they only dream early, just before waking up. The truth is you have one dream for every 90 minutes of sleep.

Luke 16:10 says that he who is faithful with little will be entrusted with much. If you want more dreams and prophetic dreams and the ability to remember your dreams, then you must begin by taking your dreams a little more seriously.

When you first fall asleep, you enter the deepest state of sleep. Imagine yourself on a high-dive diving board 32 feet above the water. As you fall asleep, you dive down to the bottom of the pool, where you are in a state of low consciousness but still able to dream. The longer you sleep, the closer you swim toward the surface and the more conscious you become. This is why you are more likely to remember your dreams just before waking, when you are in a state of REM sleep but not as deeply asleep as earlier in the night.

Think about this for a second: if you have three to five dreams a night and live to be 100 years old, you could potentially have 182,500 dreams throughout your entire life. That's a lot of data.

To become more aware of your dreams, it's important to recognize their value and the information they carry. This is where keeping a dream journal comes in. Whether it's a physical notebook or a folder in your note-taking app on your phone, make sure to write down your dreams as soon as you wake up. In the morning, take a moment to invite the Holy Spirit to help you process the dream. As you do so, you may find that additional details come to mind, and you may even gain insight or interpretation into some aspects of the dream.

Exporting your dreams from your memory to your journal and processing them with the Holy Spirit is the system for stewarding them. When you know a dream is from the Lord, but the details aren't clear as to how they translate, this is when you can share it with a trusted friend or minister who is filled with the Holy Spirit; and it helps if they are prophetic or have the gift of discernment.

INTERPRETING DREAMS

It's important to keep in mind that not all of your dreams require interpretation. Six sources can transmit information to your soul and influence your dreams while you sleep:

1. God
2. Your body
3. Your soul
4. Your spirit
5. The devil
6. Other people, spirits, or external factors

By being aware of these potential sources, you can discern which dreams may hold significant meaning and require further interpretation and which may result from other influences.

Let me share an example from my life: I once went through a season of dark and demonic dreams. Instead of trying to interpret the dreams, I focused on identifying how they got in. I would listen to Christian metal while lifting weights at the gym during this time. However, I later discovered that one of my playlists contained bands that were not Christian, and some of these bands had demonic spirits attached to their music. Even though I wasn't focusing on the lyrics, these spirits entered my soul through the music.

Art can act as a portal or gateway to the soul, and music can be a spiritual bridge connecting other realms to our earthly existence. In my case, my music choices had opened a demonic portal. The solution was simple: I repented and stopped listening to that playlist. As a result, the demonic dreams ceased.

Discerning the source of your dreams is crucial. If you are in a state of sin or compromise, you cannot trust the integrity of your dreams. Likewise, if you are not a follower of Jesus, you may be unable to determine the reliability of the information you receive.

DREAM ENCYCLOPEDIAS

Interpreting a dream is a similar process to receiving a prophetic word from the Lord. It requires listening attentively and discerning what God is saying. It's crucial not to rely on our good ideas or other people's theories when interpreting dreams. For this reason, I'm not a fan of using dream encyclopedias as the primary source for dream interpretation or randomly Googling numbers and symbols to interpret dreams.

For example, a dream encyclopedia may suggest that a car represents ministry, but God may be using the car in your dream to symbolize an important relationship or marriage. It's important to listen to God when interpreting your dreams and to bring all other dream interpretation resources to Him as you process what He is trying to communicate.

If you decide to use a dream encyclopedia, make sure it's written by a recognized spirit-filled minister rather than a new-age practitioner. You don't want to unknowingly adopt occult practices such as numerology or astrology into your faith walk with Jesus.

If you choose to read a Christian dream encyclopedia, I suggest doing so initially outside of interpreting your dreams. Instead, read it with an open mind and allow the Holy Spirit to bring various aspects to mind when interpreting future dreams. Remember that dream interpretation is a process of working through a mystery with the Holy Spirit. If done correctly, it can help you solve mysteries while deepening your relationship and intimacy with the Lord.

DREAM IMPOSTERS

Source number 6 also acknowledges that our dreams can be influenced by other people, spirits, and agencies. However, I advise against inviting, encouraging, or celebrating such behavior. The dream realm is vulnerable to manipulation; some individuals access it without God's will. It is prevalent in practices such as witchcraft and the occult. Unfortunately, even some Christians have incorporated principles from these practices.

I have had apostles and prophets come to me in my dreams, and I have even had Jesus come to me in my dreams. It is wonderful, memorable, and worth celebrating, but never have I had apostles and prophets attempting to access me through the dream realm. When this happened, it was because the Lord willed and enabled it.

I knew someone who had experiences with his wife appearing to him in his dreams, but he eventually realized that the woman he was seeing was not his wife. With the Lord's guidance and discernment, he discovered that a deceptive spirit had taken on the form of his wife.

About 20 years ago, a heresy permeated a small section of the more mystical church where individuals claimed that Jesus was romantically appearing to them. However, this "Jesus" was not the real Jesus but an incubus spirit that led to a heretical movement in the church, promoting inappropriate encounters with Jesus. These individuals misinterpreted and took verses out of context, such as those from the Song of Solomon, to support their beliefs. It's crucial to understand that just because someone appears in your dream it does not necessarily mean it's them, and the same goes for when you visit someone in a dream—it's usually not you.

ASTRAL PROJECTION

Astral projection, also known as an out-of-body experience (OBE), is an experience in which an individual's consciousness or awareness appears to leave their physical body and travel to an astral plane or dimension. This experience is often described as feeling like a separation of the physical body and the consciousness or soul. During an astral projection, the individual may feel like they are floating, flying, or traveling through a different plane of existence. They may also report seeing or encountering other entities or beings in this alternate reality.

High-level witches, sorceresses, and occultists can not only hack dreams but can also astral-project themselves outside the dream realm and project themselves into people's homes, workplaces, and even bedrooms. It is a form of supernatural breaking and entering, which is sinful and wrong.

There is a significant amount of teaching in the church on traveling in the spirit, which draws on biblical examples of bilocation. However, some of these teachings may borrow principles from new-age practices regarding methodology, which is concerning. It is worth noting that the individuals I have known who have experienced bilocation and traveling in the spirit did not follow a formula from a book. These were sovereign and God-ordered experiences.

Many of the teachings on spirit travel that I have seen appear to be focused on stimulating the soul and practicing leaving the body or bilocating through some love-based meditation. It is basically a repackaging of astral projection. Honestly, we really shouldn't be obsessed with exporting our spirits from our bodies, and the fascination with doing so would seem to be somewhat Gnostic, considering that the Gnostics believed the body was bad and the spirit was good. Love your body, stay in your body, take care of your body, and use your body. After all, Jesus put your spirit in your body in the first place, so deal with it.

If you are experiencing issues with someone projecting into your environment through astral projection, it may be due to a soul tie or attachment. Seeking ministry and breaking any soul ties can help address this issue, and it may also be necessary to forbid the person from visiting you in this way.

DREAM HACKING

The most awe-inspiring dreams have been recounted by Paul Keith Davis, Bob Jones, and Bobby Conner, where they met each other in a realm beyond imagination. Their recollection of encounters and exhilarating adventures experienced together is remarkable. It's incredible to fathom that the dream realm is indeed a tangible realm where people can meet and receive information and revelations that can alter the course of their lives.

One of the most riveting stories I've ever heard is when Bobby Conner found himself in Peru, in a dream, preaching the gospel to a remote village. He journeyed through the village on a llama's back, crossing a riverbed made of reddish clay. Upon waking from the dream, Bobby was surprised to find his pants hanging on the bathroom door, covered in red clay, and llama hair in the crotch. It was an undeniable proof that his dream was indeed a reality.

It's amazing to think such incredible things are possible, but Bobby doesn't usually divulge the secret methods of making such dreams happen. Even when teaching supernatural dreams, he focuses on bringing people back to the word of God and emphasizing intimacy with Christ. Some have criticized him, thinking he keeps secrets that could equip people to do what he does, but in reality his message is far more significant than any method.

As someone who has known Bobby for 34 years and has had the privilege of having him visit our church every year since my installation as a pastor, I can confidently say that Bobby doesn't believe in "hacking" the dream realm or the supernatural realm. In fact, through my conversations with him and observing his life, it's clear that the key to his supernatural encounters lies in his deep fellowship with Christ and unwavering obedience to Him. Bobby's emphasis is always on seeking intimacy with God, and it's from this place that the incredible things he experiences become possible.

Some individuals use these powerful stories of dream encounters to justify their so-called "dream hacks." They will scour new-age blogs and forums online, copying and pasting methods for manipulating the dream realm to bring about changes in this physical world. Often, they will even throw in out-of-context Bible verses to give their methods a veneer of legitimacy.

However, it's important to take a moment to define what it means to "hack" something. In simple terms, to hack means to gain access to something in an unconventional or unauthorized way. If someone were to hack into your email, for instance, they would be accessing it through a backdoor or exploit without your permission or knowledge. This should not be encouraged or promoted in any realm, including the dream realm.

It's important to understand that teaching others how to access and manipulate other people's dreams is not only contrary to the word of God, but it can also lead to serious problems. There are two potential dangers associated with this type of teaching. First, it's possible that individuals who claim to have had encounters with others in their dreams may have accessed a counterfeit realm. By manipulating their intent and authority, they may have created a dream that merely reflects their preconceptions and biases rather than receiving genuine revelation from God.

Second, in a worse case, these individuals may have unwittingly entered into a demonic dream, receiving teachings from a false spirit that undermines the word and character of God.

I have personally had to engage in countless conversations with people deceived by new age teachings on dreams, helping them discern that their dream was not from God. I've chatted with people who saw apocalyptic situations, ministers in sin, new theology, even new technologies.

Discerning whether a dream is from God or not, can be challenging, but there are some key principles to keep in mind. First and foremost, any dream that goes against the character and nature of God, as revealed in the Bible, should be rejected. Additionally, dreams that focus solely on the self and personal gain are unlikely to be from God. True dreams from God often come with a sense of peace and a confirmation in your spirit. They may also contain specific, prophetic messages or revelations that align with God's will and plan for your life.

Lastly, it's crucial to consider if the dream aligns with your character and capabilities. It's easy to get carried away with grandiose plans that are beyond our abilities or don't align with our values. Seeking confirmation and guidance from mature Christians is vital in this process, as they can provide valuable insight and help us identify any potential blind spots. Sometimes we can get caught up in the excitement of a dream and lose sight of whether it's from God or not. It's important to stay grounded and seek wise counsel to avoid unhealthy hysteria and ensure we align with God's will.

Ultimately, prayer and intimacy with God are essential in developing the discernment needed to distinguish between dreams that come from God and those that do not. It's important to remember that God will engage with you in your dreams.

LUCID DREAMING

Lucid dreaming is a state of dreaming in which the dreamer becomes aware they are dreaming and can exert some degree of control over the dream environment and storyline. In a lucid dream, the dreamer is conscious of their own participation in the dream and may be able to manipulate the dream's plot, setting, and characters. Lucid dreams are not necessarily evil; they can be spontaneous and fun, and if you are properly framing the night with the blood of Jesus and declaring your intent that your spirit be available and accessible only to the Holy Spirit as you sleep, that goes a long way. The problem is that lucid dreams can be induced through various techniques. In fact, you can buy a lucid-dreaming helmet on Amazon for 20 dollars that will play a sound or flash subtle lights to bring you to consciousness while remaining in REM sleep.

Lucid dreaming is considered powerful because it allows the dreamer to control and manipulate the dream experience consciously. This can be particularly empowering because in a regular dream, the dreamer often feels at the mercy of the dream's unpredictable and sometimes frightening events. In a lucid dream, however, the dreamer can exert some degree of control over the dream's environment, characters, and storyline, allowing them to explore and experience things that might not be possible in waking life.

People believe that in lucid dreams, they can do a wide range of things, such as:

1. Overcome fears and phobias by confronting them in a safe dream environment.

2. Practice new skills and hobbies without the risks or consequences of failure.

3. Explore creative ideas and solutions by using the dream state as a mental playground.

4. Experience new sensations and pleasures that might not be possible in waking life, such as flying or visiting fantastical locations.

5. Engage in spiritual or mystical experiences, such as meeting with deceased loved ones or connecting with higher states of consciousness.

Lucid dreaming can potentially have negative consequences, and it's important to approach it cautiously. Some people have reported unreliable and even dangerous experiences while attempting to engage in lucid dreaming intentionally. This can occur because it's difficult to determine the accuracy of the dream data, and external forces, such as demonic interference, can interfere with the dreamer's control.

For instance, some have reported being deceived into thinking they had control while being manipulated by negative forces, similar to how a robot drives a Tesla. I have had experiences in which I believed I had control over my dreams, only to wake up and regret my decisions. Through reflection and guidance from the Holy Spirit, I realized that I had been deceived into thinking that I was driving the dream, leading me to feel ashamed and as if I had committed a sin upon waking.

It's crucial to approach the dream realm with honor and submission to the will of the Father. This involves pleading the blood of Jesus, declaring that only the Father's intentions be fulfilled, and immediately rejecting any dream that feels negative, off, or evil.

NIGHT SCHOOL IN HELL

I once had the privilege of spending time with a former warlock who had been saved by supernatural means and came from several generations of witches. During our conversation, he revealed that he had to change his name and relocate to Seattle due to the danger his conversion posed. During our talk, he revealed that when he was a child, a demon would visit him every night and lead him to a classroom in the spiritual realm. The demon would teach him what he needed to know to become a high priest there. I found this story intriguing.

According to him, the devil comes to steal, kill, and destroy, except when he is grooming someone. This particular demon had given him a set of laws and rules to live by, aiming to preserve him rather than destroy him. For example, he was not to use drugs or overindulge in alcohol.

However, not all those who come to people in the middle of the night are ambassadors of darkness. In 1 Samuel 3, God calls Samuel three times during the night, and on each occasion, Samuel mistakes the voice for that of Eli, the high priest who raised him. Only after the third call does Eli realize it is God calling Samuel and advises him to answer. This pivotal moment marks the beginning of Samuel's prophetic ministry, which would play a significant role in the history of Israel.

JESUS VISITS PEOPLE AT NIGHT!

In an extraordinary account shared by a Middle Eastern missionary, Jesus appeared to a man in the region every night for a month and asked him to write down His words. The missionary revealed that Jesus shared the entire book of John with the man, who lived over 30 miles outside a Middle Eastern city known for its heavy use of opium.

This incredible story was recounted by "Yazid," a pseudonym given by McLean Bible Church Pastor David Platt during The Gospel Coalition's "Something Needs to Change Simulcast" a few years ago. Yazid and his wife are working in a part of the Middle East where it is illegal to share the gospel, and even discussing the spread of the gospel is a life-threatening activity.

Despite the challenges, Yazid and his wife are dedicated to sharing the gospel with Muslims who have never heard it and planting churches in the region. According to Yazid, "God is moving inside the Middle East with dreams, visions, and personal visitations."

Even today, the supernatural realms of the kingdom of light and darkness attempt to visit people at night. This generation is bombarded with distractions and temptations, magic, the occult, and spiritism, making it difficult to figure out what is true and right.

Satan, the enemy of our souls, works tirelessly to keep people from seeking a relationship with God. He uses every tool at his disposal to distract people from God's truth and power and lead them to deception and destruction.

Jesus wants to come to you. He wants to awaken the potential of the night. As you dedicate yourself to the Lord and invite His kingdom to come and His will to be done, get ready as His supernatural glory invades your thoughts and dreams. There will be things you know that you know, and don't know how you know. There will be wisdom that you will begin to walk in. A peace that you cannot explain. And all of this will be because you have been awakened to your authority, and you have taken back the night hours for the glory of God.

WHEN YOU WAKE UP

Just as important as sleeping is waking up. As the sun rises, you wake up to a new day, eager to start fresh and make the most of the divine opportunities that the Lord will open up before you. But before diving into the busyness of the day, take a moment to carve out your morning discipline. In the same way that you dedicated the night to the Lord, be sure to likewise dedicate your morning, sanctifying it, setting it apart unto the Lord.

Begin with prayer, connect with God, and give Him thanks for the blessing of life. Take time to commune with the Lord by sharing your joys and concerns with Him, asking for guidance and wisdom for the day ahead. As you pray, take time to receive the peace and comfort needed to engage the day.

Next, open your Bible and read a passage, taking time to reflect on its meaning and how it applies to your life. Don't speed-read. Meditate on the words, seeking to understand God's will for them and how they prophetically apply to your own life and faith. As you read, take time to feel the word of God at work within your spirit, growing your confidence and resolve in Jesus.

Strive to be disciplined and intentional with your morning. Recognize that this time is a priority in your day. The benefits of this time will extend beyond the morning hours, helping you to be more focused, productive, and peaceful throughout the day.

If you begin your day by diving deep into the heart of God, no matter what storm rages against the surface, you will be sheltered and protected from its influence.

Morning Prayer

Dear God, thank You for this new and incredible day You gave me. I choose to rejoice and be glad in it. As I begin my day, I ask for Your wisdom and favor. Help me to make the most of every opportunity that comes my way. I thank You that Your hand is at work in my life, and I declare that I trust Your perfect plan. I pray for Your protection and provision for me this day and that You would help me to be salt and light to those around me. Thank You for Your unfailing love. I receive it by faith, in Jesus' name, amen.

Goodnight

As you can see, the night is a time of powerful open-heaven encounters, and the Lord invites you to reclaim it. The devil did not create the night to torment people; our mighty God ordained it as a time of spiritual renewal and restoration. The time has come for you to wield your authority in Christ and raise your expectations of what God can do at night.

Prepare your heart for each night to become a supernatural encounter with the divine, a time of revival and awakening. As you surrender your spirit and soul to the Lord in preparation for sleep, anticipate that the Lord will impart divine intelligence to fulfill your kingdom assignments.

Don't forget to keep a record of what you learn and journal your dream revelations. Allow the Holy Spirit to guide you in processing your insights and prepare you for a powerful upgrade in your spiritual walk. In this revelation, you will unlock the secrets of the night and embrace the supernatural destiny God has for you.

ACTIVATION PRAYER

Heavenly Father, I come before You in the mighty name of my Lord and Savior, Jesus Christ. I declare His Lordship over my life and over tonight.

Father, I declare that tonight, Your kingdom will come and Your will will be done. Please help me align my thoughts and actions with Your divine purpose. I declare, I have the mind of Christ.

I ask for Your protection against the schemes of the enemy. Keep me safe from his attacks and shield me from deception. I also ask that You protect me from counterfeit dreams and false portals. May I only encounter true visions and dreams from You, O Lord.

I pray for an outpouring of true dreams from Yahweh. May I experience dreams of heaven, where I can glimpse Your glory and majesty. May I dream of angels who carry out Your divine will and surround me with Your protection. And may I have dreams from Jesus, who speaks to me in love and guides me into truth.

Father, I thank You for Your faithfulness and Your love for me. I trust in Your promises, and I believe that You will answer my prayers according to Your will. In Jesus' name, I pray. Amen.

CHAPTER EIGHT

THE BATTLE FOR THE EARTH

"You said in your heart, 'I will ascend to heaven; above the stars of God I will set my throne on high; I will sit on the mount of assembly in the far reaches of the north.'"

—ISAIAH 14:13 ESV

THE SUPERNATURAL CULTURE

One of the biggest challenges facing the church in the near future is the rise of supernaturalism in society. The days of mainstream secularism and atheism are over; more and more people are embracing the paranormal, ancestral living, and shaman medicine. The reliance on reason without any supernatural beliefs is fading away, and supernatural beings are now a part of mainstream culture, including entertainment, news, and education.

Secular humanism, which rejects supernatural beliefs and relies solely on reason, has been

relegated to the grave and buried six feet under. The once-revered figure of Richard Dawkins, a prominent atheist and advocate of secular humanism, has been overshadowed by the likes of Harry Potter. In a remarkable turn of events, paranormal phenomena, once thought to be confined to the realm of comic books and television shows like *The X-Files,* are now the subject of serious investigation by the CIA and FBI, and the results of these investigations are being declassified for public scrutiny.

For example, the U.S. Congress passed a law requiring the director of national intelligence to report on UFOs, released on June 25, 2021. The report disclosed 144 incidents of unidentified aerial phenomena that military personnel had observed over the years. While I don't believe that these unidentified aerial phenomena are necessarily paranormal, it's evident that supernatural beings are becoming more prevalent in American culture.

As Christians, we must exercise discernment and be prepared to confront and resist demonic influences that may seek to infiltrate our homes, churches, and Christian education institutions. We must ground ourselves in sound doctrine and theology and walk in the gift of the discerning of spirits to handle the challenges of a culture continuing to boldly embrace evil.

Demonic beings will become more prevalent in American culture, and as Christians, we must exercise discernment to keep them out of our homes, churches, and Christian education institutions. As our culture enters a new dispensation of enchantment, I am concerned that the church has become too secularized for the world. Our attempts to integrate gospel-centered dynamics into cultural conversations have failed, and society has embraced elements of supernaturalism in every aspect of culture.

The entertainment industry, news networks, and schools are all being inundated by the tide of magic, and unfortunately, most modern-day believers lack the necessary doctrine, theology, and discernment to prevent supernatural influences from infiltrating our domains. We will soon witness modern-day celebrities performing miracles, exorcisms, and resurrections. On October 29, 2013, magician Chris Angel attempted to raise the dead using a real human corpse on his Spike TV show "BeLIEve." Although the attempt failed, I am certain this will not be the last attempt of its kind.

The supernatural is poised to take center stage, and the pressing question we must ask ourselves is whether we are prepared. It brings to mind the story of the prophet Elijah and his powerful confrontation with the false prophets of Baal on Mount Carmel. In a public showdown, Elijah faced off against 450 demon-possessed prophets of the god Baal. Could we be facing similar modern-day battles between the forces of darkness and the forces of light?

As followers of Christ, we must equip ourselves to resist and confront the deceivingly attractive forces of darkness. We must root ourselves in sound doctrine and a Christ-centered theology. To do so, we also need to be baptized in the fire of the Holy Spirit to such an extent that we can not only confront but also defeat and dismantle their authority.

A PORTAL HAS BEEN OPENED

Decades ago, Bobby Conner, Paul Keith Davis, Rick Joyner, and Bob Jones sounded the alarm to the church of the impending danger. They all had visions and dreams of portals opening in the United States, unleashing hordes of demons and other entities that would flood the country. Paul Keith Davis warned, "We are on the brink of witnessing third-world evil in first-world nations."

After hearing about the warnings from the men mentioned above, I connected with a friend consulting for the public school district in our neighboring city. His Christian non-profit had established a unique relationship with the district, allowing the regional church to come together and revive the failing sports department. The non-profit operated excellently and had an office in each public school.

One day, a coach from the middle school contacted my friend in distress. A young student exhibited superhuman strength and threw other children through the air and to the ground during recess. The coach had managed to detain the student and bring him to his office, where he displayed clear symptoms of demon possession. The coach, having no experience in deliverance, begged my friend to come as soon as possible. Upon arrival, the diagnosis was confirmed, as the boy would react strongly and negatively to the mention of Jesus. Step by step, guided by the Holy Spirit, my friend walked through a systematic deliverance process, even though he had never done it before and had never received any formal training. Ultimately, the young boy was radically set free by the power of God.

The following day, the coach followed up with the boy to check his progress. The boy revealed that while walking to school the previous day, he was followed by a large black dog that eventually chased him and then jumped *into* him.

Apparently, we are witnessing the manifestation of third-world evil in America. A portal has been opened, and it's unclear if we can close it. It's imperative that we acknowledge the gravity of the situation and become vigilant gatekeepers. We must be baptized in the Holy Spirit and adequately trained to cast out demons.

THE PROBLEM AND THE GOOD NEWS

As the pastor of Seattle Revival Center, we hosted a Sunday night series in which our congregation submitted popular topics for discussion, and people voted on them. I covered a broad range of subjects, from gender theory to hybrid beings. My sermon on aliens and UFOs was one topic I expected to be silly.

Interestingly, I had an unusual dream the week before I preached on the topic. In the dream, I was staying in a strange home and woke up to find a dragon running up and through the rafters overhead. The dragon resembled a Chinese depiction of a dragon and was around eight feet long, roughly the height of a large dog but longer. I was not afraid when I saw it, and it was more like watching a rat scurrying through the rafters. On the wall, I noticed a star chart of the constellations and the yin-yang symbol. At that moment, I realized beings were standing at the foot of my bed. These beings had large heads, eyes, and no nose, and it was unclear whether they had a mouth. They seemed to exude an aura of pure evil and terror.

I cried out, "I rebuke you in Jesus' name!" and immediately awoke from the dream.

When I taught about aliens, I approached the topic from the perspective that the aliens themselves were demonic and that the UFOs were a form of advanced technology. I shared true accounts of attempted abductions where people rebuked the aliens in the name of Jesus and the beings fled. During the message, some people walked out of the meeting, and many online were offended that I so easily dismissed these alien beings as evil without considering the possibility that they might be created beings from another planet in need of evangelism. Some may have even taken inspiration from the Catholic Church's initiative to train intergalactic missionaries.

Since that sermon, my opinion on the matter has evolved. As I reflect on my dream, it seems as though the Lord was teaching me something about the nature of these "aliens." I don't believe they are demons, but they are evil beings in a different category, more similar to the dragon I saw in my dream. They are wicked overseers who must still flee when rebuked in the name of Jesus, but their job description may differ from that of typical earth-bound demons.

One issue in the church is that we have reduced all spiritual beings into two categories: angels and demons. However, the Bible never does that. Throughout the Bible, we find a variety of spiritual beings, both good and evil, with different job descriptions and functions.

In many Christian circles, any spiritual being that belongs to God is considered an angel, but the word *angel* means "messenger." Angels are described as awesome beings, appearing as humans without wings, and are found in Genesis through Revelation. However, the Bible mentions other supernatural beings employed by God, some of whom have wings. For instance, in Ezekiel 1, a creature is described that looks like a wheel but is actually a living creature covered in eyes. Thomas Aquinas, in his *Summa Theologica* I:61:4, explains the different types of angels. He identifies this wheel-like creature as the ophanim, a type of angel that is closest to God. He says that they are the immediate objects of the divine knowledge, which means that they are the things that God knows most directly. He also says that they have eyes all around, which means that they are perfectly cognizant of all things. The kingdom of God has a diverse cast of beings and creatures; the same can be true of those outside of Yahweh's team. For example, the nations at the tower of Babel were given a cast of divine beings, which are addressed in Deuteronomy 32:8-9 (ESV):

> *When the Most High gave to the nations their inheritance, when he divided mankind, he fixed the borders of the peoples according to the number of the sons of God. But the Lord's portion is his people, Jacob his allotted heritage.*

Jeffrey Tigay addresses what is taking place here in his commentary of Deuteronomy:

> The idea stated in the variant reading that the number of nations equals the number of "sons of the divine" suggests that each of these beings is paired with a nation. Jewish sources of the Hellenistic and Talmudic periods elaborate on this

picture, indicating that God appointed divine beings to govern the nations on His behalf.

Ben Sira paraphrases our passage as follows:

In dividing up the peoples of all the world, Over every people He appointed a ruler, But the Lord's portion is Israel.

The "rulers" are Ben Sira's equivalent of Deuteronomy's "sons of the divine." The book of Daniel, from the same period as Ben Sira, refers to them as "governors" or "princes" (Heb. sarim) and describes them as angelic patrons and champions of various nations.[1]

It's important to note that these "gods" mentioned in Deuteronomy 32:8-9 are not necessarily demons. They are divine beings that should not be worshiped by the Israelites, as stated in the first Ten Commandments in Exodus 20:3 (ESV): *"You shall have no other gods before me."*

The Bible portrays a diverse range of spiritual beings, including demons, angels, and others that are difficult to classify. Additionally, there are principalities, powers, rulers of the darkness of this world, spiritual wickedness in high places, and gods. The resistance facing the church and nations is not a matter of flesh and blood but a spiritual battle against these entities.

DRAGONS

The fact that DreamWorks is teaching kids how to train dragons is not coincidental. The culture is being prepared for a future without barriers between hell and earth, and hybrid creatures are commonplace. The next chapter will explore God's response to this end-times agenda. It's safe to say that until His return, we must learn how to stand firm in our faith.

Dragons have been a significant part of many ancient civilizations and are even a part of our Judaic roots. The well-known Sunday school tale of "Jonah and the Whale" may be more accurately translated as "Jonah and the Chaos Dragon." Bible scholar Scott Noegel explains the Hebrew word choice and understanding of this in his article "Jonah and Leviathan: Inner Biblical Allusions and the Problem with Dragons," published in the scholarly journal *Henoch* 37:2 (2015). He and other modern-day scholars suggest that the sea monster that swallowed Jonah for three days was some form of a dragon-like creature.

This interpretation is essential to the prophetic implications of the story. The narrative is a prophetic drama that points to Jesus, who, like Jonah, was swallowed by the belly of the chaos dragon, Hades. However, Jesus was not defeated and digested but rather defeated the dragon from within and, on the third day, emerged victorious with the keys to death and hell. This understanding of Jonah and the Chaos Dragon story helps us understand the prophetic significance of Jesus' resurrection.

In ancient Europe, dragons were often portrayed as terrifying beasts associated with evil and destruction. They were often depicted as the enemy of knights and were defeated in epic battles. In ancient Greece and Rome, dragons were viewed as power symbols and often associated with the gods. They were also seen as guardians of treasure and were often defeated by heroes. In ancient Mesoamerican cultures, such as the Maya and Aztecs, dragons were associated with the underworld and were viewed as powerful and dangerous creatures.

The Chinese had a different perspective on dragons compared to what a biblical worldview would recommend. In China, dragons were not seen as symbols of the doorway to hell but rather as symbols of power, good fortune, and prosperity. The ancient Chinese believed that dragons were benevolent creatures associated with the emperor. They were believed to have control over weather systems and could bring rain and ideal weather patterns to yield abundant harvests.

Additionally, dragons were believed to be beings that could grant fertility. According to Chinese culture, dragons were not viewed as animals but as highly magical, intelligent, shapeshifting noble beings. They lived deep in the seas and brought rain with them. When they left their aquatic dwellings to fly across the sky, they could cause gales and storms.

Dragon Coffee

Do you recognize this dragon?

You may think, "That's not a dragon; that's the Starbucks Mermaid!" However, the Starbucks Queen is not a two-tailed siren or a mermaid, like the Seattle coffee franchise claims. She is a Melusine, a fish-like being that is a serpent, dragon-like from the waist down, has two tails, and is human-like from the waist up. Melusines are believed to be principalities that govern fresh waters, considered equally haunted and holy.

So who is the two-tailed serpent on your favorite green coffee cup? Legend has it that she was a cursed maiden who lived in a forest and was discovered by the Duke of Aquitaine, Raymond. He found her in the woods and asked her to be his wife. She agreed but warned him never to bother her on Saturdays because that was when she bathed. Raymond initially agreed but eventually became suspicious and spied on her while she bathed. He was shocked at what he saw, and the Melusine caught him spying. She flew into a rage and turned into a dragon before leaving her husband.

Yes, you read that correctly. The two-tailed Starbucks mermaid is a dragon believed to haunt various fresh waters in Europe today. Is she a demon? Probably not. Is she a ruling being in a second-heaven realm with a certain amount of authority in a particular territory? Perhaps.

Let's cross cultures and apply a Chinese worldview to this particular entity. Suppose dragons are symbolic of majesty and prosperity. Could there be a connection between appeasing this dragon and the average annual income reported by Starbucks, which is around 25 billion dollars? Is there any other way to explain a company making such an enormous profit by selling burnt coffee?

ALIENS

In a 2016 interview with *The Hollywood Reporter*, Steven Spielberg expressed his fascination with the question of whether we are alone in the universe and his desire to see a story where aliens are just as surprised to find us as we are to find them. However, the reality is that aliens will not be surprised to find us. This idea that aliens are unaware of our existence is a romanticized notion that does not reflect the reality of the occult and extraterrestrial phenomena. The truth is, these beings already know exactly who we are.

Aleister Crowley, a British occultist, writer, and ceremonial magician known for his involvement in various occult and magical societies, as well as his philosophy of Thelema, claimed to have made contact with extraterrestrial entities through his magical practices.

In 1918, Crowley attempted to create a dimensional vortex, a portal that would bridge the gap between two realms—the world of the seen and the unseen. The ritual, known as the Amalantrah Working, was deemed successful when a spiritual portal opened, and Crowley claimed that an actual extraterrestrial-like being appeared through the rift. He called the being "Lam" and even drew a portrait. Interestingly, the sketch he drew of Lam resembles how aliens are commonly portrayed in modern times.

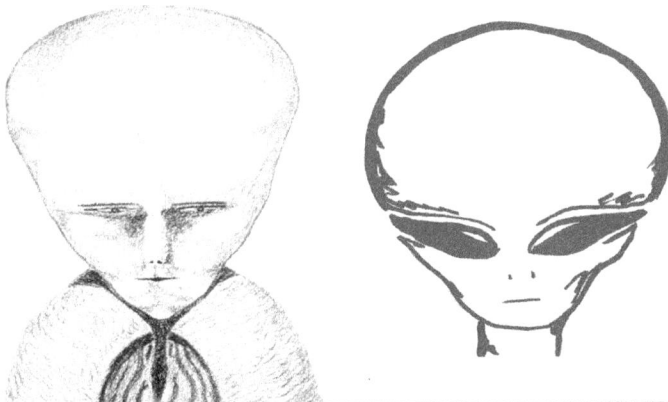

Left: *Aleister Crowley's 1918 drawing of "LAM"*
Right: *Artist's rendering of a grey alien*

Remember that when Crowley drew his sketch of the being he called "Lam," there were no widely accepted depictions of extraterrestrials in pop culture. Yet his drawing closely resembles the common depiction of "Grey" aliens. This type of alien is typically described as having a small, slender body, a pear-shaped head larger than its body, gray-colored skin with a smooth texture, large black almond-shaped eyes, and no visible nose or mouth. Some depictions also include small nostrils and a small slit for a mouth.

Interestingly, Crowley died in 1947, the same year as the Roswell crash, Kenneth Arnold's sighting of nine flying saucers near Mount Rainier, and the beginning of reported sightings of aliens worldwide.

Recently, the evangelization of hallucinogenics like DMT through cultural influencers like Tim Ferris, Joe Rogan, and Michael Pollan has led to an increase in those who were traditionally atheists finding themselves propelled into the spirit world at breakneck speed, hurtling through the same portal that Crowley accessed all those years ago. What once required ritualistic preparation and dedication to the dark arts is now accessible to spiritual seekers who lack context and understanding.

In May 2020, health columnist Kashmira Gander wrote an article in *Newsweek* titled "Taking DMT Can Lead to Experiences Similar to Those Reported by People Who Claim to Have Been Abducted by Aliens, Study Shows." This highlights the dangers of unguided exploration of these realms and the potential for individuals to encounter entities they are ill-equipped to understand or engage with safely.

The article reports on a study by researchers at Johns Hopkins University who analyzed the accounts of 2,561 individuals who claimed to have had encounters with paranormal entities resembling "Greys." The study found that DMT produced an out-of-body experience in which these individuals felt as if they were observing the beings from a distance.

The researchers concluded that DMT-induced encounters with aliens shared many commonalities with non-drug-related encounters with entities, including those described in religious, near-death, and alien abduction contexts. The article states that almost every respondent had an emotional response to meeting the alien-like being, with 41 percent reporting feelings of fear. However, the most prominent emotions respondents felt were love, kindness, and joy. Additionally, 69 percent of respondents stated that the alien-like being gave them a message, and nearly one-fifth received a prediction about the future.

The focus of the conversation around extraterrestrial life is shifting from the possibility of life on other planets to the possibility of life in other realms and parallel dimensions. Some theories suggest that psychedelic experiences could offer a means of encountering these beings. Dr. Rick Strassman's study on DMT found that participants reported encounters with intelligent beings they believed to be extraterrestrial, often describing them as having a spiritual or otherworldly quality and communicating through telepathy or nonverbal means. The possibility of encountering extraterrestrial life through psychedelic experiences is now being explored in scientific and spiritual communities.

When it comes to the topic of aliens, I clarify that there is no evidence to support the existence of Martians or UFOs. However, there are interdimensional rulers and principalities that resemble the "greys" depicted in popular culture. These ETs do not travel in spaceships but access our realm through portals that individuals open.

Comedian and podcast host Joe Rogan has been a vocal proponent of psychedelic substances, including DMT, and has discussed his encounters with these otherworldly beings on his show. He interviewed Dr. Rick Strassman, who conducted a DMT study and shared his experiences meeting intelligent entities that he believes to be extraterrestrial or interdimensional. These experiences have profoundly impacted Rogan's understanding of consciousness and spirituality.

LOCH NESS MONSTER

As we delve into the realm of paranormal interdimensional entities, one cannot help but wonder whether the Loch Ness monster, a cryptid steeped in folklore and legend, could fall under this category. The study of this elusive creature is undeniably fascinating, as it encompasses a rich history steeped in spiritual and supernatural beliefs.

The earliest documented encounter with the Loch Ness monster was chronicled in Book II, Chapter XXVII of St. Adomnán's *Vita Columbae*. This historical account follows the life of St. Columba, an exceptional sixth-century Irish abbot who journeyed to Scotland to convert the Picts to Christianity. While traveling, St. Columba encountered the creature and even admonished it. St. Adomnán's retelling of the story vividly details and offers an intriguing glimpse into the earliest known interaction with the elusive beast.

According to St. Adomnán, St. Columba and his companions were traveling near the river Ness when they heard rumors from the locals about someone who had just recently been attacked by a river monster. When they found the men who were burying the young boy, they learned that the monster had snatched him while swimming in the river. The creature had viciously bitten him, and although some men tried to save him, it was too late.

Unfazed by the story, St. Columba ordered his colleague Lugne Mocumin to swim across the river and retrieve a boat from the other side. As Mocumin swam, the monster emerged from the depths of the river with a deafening roar, its huge mouth open wide, and began to pursue him. The saintly entourage was afraid as the creature closed in on Mocumin, who was desperately swimming for his life.

St. Columba quickly raised his arms in the air, made a sign of the cross, rebuking the monster in Jesus' name, and commanded it to leave Mocumin alone and go away.

Remarkably, the creature immediately obeyed Columba and retreated into the river's depths, leaving Mocumin unharmed.

The Scottish Highlands, where the freshwater loch is located and where the original sightings of the Loch Ness monster were reported, has a rich history of being a hub for mythical and monstrous creatures, as documented in ancient manuscripts. Legends recount a plethora of strange and malevolent creatures in the region, ranging from hell-hounds of the underworld to fearsome dragons capable of breathing fire. One such tale recounts the heroic exploits of Fraser of Glenvackie, who allegedly slew the last of the Scottish dragons. Despite the dragon's defeat, the river monster remained alive and thriving, lurking deep beneath the waters of Loch Ness.

The region is rife with tales of malevolent entities, including a sea dragon inhabiting the waters of Loch Ness. The presence of ancient myths surrounding shape-shifting beings known as kelpies adds another layer of intrigue. These creatures, also called water-horses, could morph into various forms, including terrifying serpentine monsters, horses, hairy humanoids, mermaid-like maidens, and more.

Their sole purpose was to lure unsuspecting victims into the depths and drown them. They are said to possess mane-like hair flowing down the back of their heads and necks, similar to that of horses.

On other occasions, the kelpie is said to appear not as a horse but as a wild, hair-covered man resembling Bigfoot. This description was famously portrayed by an 1879 incident on Bridge 39 of England's old Shropshire Union Canal. One late January night, a man and his horse were attacked by a half-human, half-ape-like creature that leaped out of the surrounding woods. Shaggy and covered in hair, this creature became known as the Man-Monkey. Interestingly, local police associated the creature's presence with the death of a man who drowned in the canal under mysterious circumstances.

While kelpie legends are associated with multiple bodies of water in Scotland, it is no coincidence that many of these stories revolve around Loch Ness. Some believe this could be attributed to the sightings of the Loch Ness monster. As for the Loch Ness monster, most likely it's not a surviving dinosaur but instead a product of ancient Celtic shamanism and occult technology. The "monster," not actually a monster at all, is most likely simply occultists who can shift their appearance into various forms, such as sea serpents, horses, and Scottish sasquatches, all empowered by demonic forces.

SASQUATCH

My family and I reside in Seattle, making this particular supernatural being a topic of interest for us. The Pacific Northwest is renowned for its breathtaking natural beauty, coffee, and Bigfoot hunting. For decades, many have ventured into our deep woods, hoping to encounter a yeti. However, it should be noted that most of us in the PNW do not believe in the existence of an ape-like creature that throws rocks at people's homes and bangs sticks against trees.

While I don't want to discount the experiences of those who claim to have seen a sasquatch, I have a different perspective on what may be happening. I believe there are two possibilities when it comes to the sasquatch phenomenon:

1. There may be demonic entities at play who are specifically haunting certain areas, or there may be individuals who have opened themselves up to the occult or other sins against God.

2. It's also possible that some of the sightings are of humans who possess shamanic or spiritual abilities and can shape-shift into a sasquatch. It is similar to the legends surrounding the Loch Ness monster, where sightings could be attributed to humans rather than physical creatures.

The sasquatch has its roots in Native American spiritism, with the name *sasquatch* coming from the Salish word *sasquits*, while the Algonquin of the north-central region refers to it as a *witiko* or wendigo. According to accounts passed down by Northwest indigenous tribes, the sasquatch is not a large skunk ape but a powerful and reclusive spiritual being with supernatural abilities. The tribes never believed sasquatch to be an animal but a malevolent supernatural entity with a lust for blood. They believed the sasquatch to be a messenger of the dead, carrying the spirits of the departed to the afterlife.

It could explain why most sasquatch encounters don't involve an actual sighting of the being but rather poltergeist-like activities. Poltergeists are traditionally defined as ghosts or supernatural beings responsible for physical disturbances such as loud noises and objects being thrown around. This is typically what occurs in the majority of sasquatch encounters.

The typical sasquatch encounter often involves several unusual occurrences, including:

1. Rocks being thrown.

2. Hearing disembodied voices.

3. Unexplained raps and knocks.

4. Sudden unpleasant odors (often described as resembling rotten eggs).

5. Objects being moved.

6. Feeling as though someone or something is watching.

All of the manifestations of the sasquatch are similar to those experienced in a typical haunted house, with the difference being that they occur in the woods. Interestingly, many sasquatch encounters are associated with locations or individuals who have opened themselves up to demonic manifestations and possession through spiritism or the occult. It is not to say that there isn't a physical form of sasquatch, but it's worth noting that Native American beliefs suggest that sasquatch is a shape-shifter, meaning the hairy beast isn't its original form.

In various cultures worldwide, including some to this day, shamans and medicine people can shape-shift. This ability is considered a gift from the spirits, and specific practices and rituals are associated with shape-shifting that vary among tribes. In some cases, drugs and other substances are used to induce a trance-like state in which they can shape-shift, while in other cases, ritual dances or other ceremonies are used to connect with the spirits and gain their power.

In summary, one could argue that sasquatches exist as vampires and werewolves do, but they are not a natural part of God's created order. Instead, they are a distorted and demonic violation of God's creation, resulting from individuals surrendering themselves to evil.

Recently, I heard a story of a young man who underwent deliverance after being tormented and possessed by a cat-like demon that took possession of his soul after he was in a room where his friends were playing with a Ouija board. During his deliverance, the demon began to manifest and speak through the man, causing his canine teeth to grow into large, sharp, cat-like fangs. After the man was delivered, his teeth returned to their normal size.

It's important that we prepare ourselves for more of these sightings and hauntings of these paranormal beings, but it's also important that we don't become impressed by them. They are not real monsters. They are just people lured in by power and are now part of a priesthood of darkness.

ON EARTH AS IT IS IN HEAVEN

In John 10:10 (NIV), Jesus reveals the devil's nature: "*The thief comes only to steal and kill and destroy; I have come that they may have life, and have it to the full.*"

The devil despises the earth and those whom the Lord has appointed to govern it. He knows that his reign on earth is limited and that his judgment is imminent. Interestingly, the Lord's Prayer is a source of great discomfort for the devil. According to Prophet Bobby Conner, witches cannot recite it, making it a useful tool for identifying them.

Let's examine the Lord's Prayer in Matthew 6:9-13 (ESV):

> *Our Father in heaven, hallowed be your name. Your kingdom come, your will be done, on earth as it is in heaven. Give us this day our daily bread, and forgive us our debts, as we also have forgiven our debtors. And lead us not into temptation but deliver us from evil. For yours is the kingdom and the power and the glory, forever. Amen.*

The Lord's Prayer points us back to the innocence of Genesis 1 and 2 before mankind rebelled against God. It also points us to restoring innocence, beauty, and unity between heaven and earth in Revelation 21 and 22. Jesus encourages us to pray for the reunification of heaven and earth, despite the pushback from the darkness. We can stand firm in knowing that this prayer will be answered, and earth will be restored to its original state.

The devil desires to make earth his home and turn it into a place indistinguishable from Hell. He has convinced himself that earth was created for him. In the past, the devil and his forces would hide in the shadows, using narratives and concepts to influence people. The famous proverb says, "The greatest trick the Devil ever pulled was convincing the world he didn't exist." However, it seems that the devil has stopped hiding and is making his move. Through American culture, Hell is advancing a seductive, rebellious, and anti-Christ program. Satan has always had a fast track to cultural influence, but it used to be secretive. Now, it is out in the open that a devil is alive and well, and his army is working hard to enforce the agenda of darkness on earth.

Celebrities put the hand sign on their eye to represent 666 over the all-seeing eye, which appears on the American dollar bill.

February 5, 2023, Sam Smith and Kim Petras performed their chart-topping song "Unholy" during the 65th Grammy Awards.

The performance was criticized for its satanic imagery and was called "full-on, openly satanic, 'What Is Going to Happen?'"

The supernatural fight between good and evil is ultimately a cosmic battle for the earth. It is not a fight between political parties but between God and Satan. Despite the present spiritual intensity within our culture, we can rest assured that the ultimate outcome of this battle is already determined. Jesus has already crushed the head of the serpent under His heel and restored authority to His body, the church, on the earth.

Revelation 20:10 (ESV) states, *"And the devil who had deceived them was thrown into the lake of fire and sulfur where the beast and the false prophet were, and they will be tormented day and night forever and ever."* It is the ultimate fate of the devil, who will be judged and thrown into his eternal punishment, the lake of fire. This judgment is often called the Great White Throne Judgment, representing the final defeat of Satan and all who have rejected God's saving love.

Although we know the end of the story and our ultimate victory through Jesus Christ, we are currently engaged in a spiritual battle against the forces of darkness. As believers, we are called to resist the devil and his temptations, standing firm in our faith and relying on God's power to overcome evil.

This supernatural battle reminds us that there is a greater reality beyond what we can see, and we can choose to align ourselves with God's kingdom or the enemy's agenda. As faithful warriors, we must fight the good fight of faith and shine the light of Christ in a dark world, being agents of God's kingdom in a broken and hurting world.

The Bible promises that in the end God's victory will be complete, and there will be a new heaven and a new earth, free from the ravages of sin and evil. In this new Eden, we will rule and reign with our messianic King, Jesus Christ. The earth will be restored to God's original design, and the celestial and terrestrial will be united. We will be united with God and His family forever, with no separation. We have a crucial role to play in preparing the earth for the return of the King, but first we must engage in a spiritual battle between darkness and light. As righteous remnants, we stand firm in our faith and boldly proclaim the good news of salvation. We refuse to waver in our pursuit of becoming more like Jesus, embracing the supernatural without hesitation or apology.

ACTIVATION PRAYER

I declare that I have the mind of Christ and that I am filled with the wisdom and discernment of King Jesus.

I declare that my home is a sanctuary of peace and joy where the Holy Spirit is welcomed, and every spirit that is not in alignment with the Holy Spirit is not welcome and must leave now in Jesus' name! I boldly declare that my family is protected by Your mighty hand and that Your angels encamp around us.

I declare that I am unapologetically supernatural, empowered by Holy Spirit to do the works that Jesus did and even greater works. Let signs, wonders, and miracles follow me wherever I go as I boldly proclaim Your truth and demonstrate Your power.

I boldly declare that I shall fear no evil, for You are with me. I have been called to drive back the darkness, preach the good news of the kingdom, and demonstrate the power of God unto salvation.

I declare that I am a soldier of light for Your army, equipped with the full armor of God to stand against the schemes of the enemy. Let me shine brightly in the darkness, bringing hope and healing to lost and broken people.

In Jesus' mighty name, amen!

NOTE

1. Jeffrey Tigay, *Deuteronomy*, qtd. in Michael S. Heiser, *Demons: What the Bible Really Says About the Powers of Darkness* (Bellingham, WA: Lexham Press, 2020), 147-148.

CHAPTER NINE

THE PRIESTHOOD

"Every Christian is not only a child of God, but also a priest of God, able to come directly into His presence without any human intermediary."

—R.C. SPROUL

On March 7, 2023, the *New York Post* reported a terrifying incident involving nearly 30 schoolgirls hospitalized after playing with Ouija boards at their school in Colombia. The girls reportedly experienced severe anxiety attacks, fainting, and other symptoms, prompting concerns about their safety. This incident came just one year after a similar episode on November 12, 2022, in which 11 students aged 13 to 17 were found passed out in a school corridor. They experienced violent vomiting, abdominal pain, and muscle spasms, with thick drool coming from their mouths. The mayor of Hato, Jose Pablo Toloza Rondón, expressed his concern, saying that the children were short of

breath when they were discovered and that these incidents happened after playing with Ouija boards.

On May 14, 2019, the Catholic publication/blog "Crux" reported on a meeting in Rome in which representatives from various Christian churches convened to discuss exorcism with the Catholic clergy. One concerning issue raised was the growing number of reports that suggest an increasing number of people are seeking possession.

Speaking to Crux, Father Enrich Junger of the Anglican Church of North America noted that while exorcisms have always been a problem, there has been a rise in voluntary possessions. He cited the popularity of Ouija boards and shamanism, in which individuals seek to attain altered states of consciousness to interact with a spirit world and channel transcendent energies, as reasons for this increase. He explained people are drawn to the perceived "power" that comes with being possessed.

According to Father Junger, many young people end up possessed or disturbed after playing games that invite dialogue with demons, while others explicitly ask to be possessed through shamanism. As a result of this increase in voluntary possession, the Catholic Church warns people against attempting exorcisms at home. They stress that exorcisms should only be performed by ordained priests with the express permission of the local bishop and only after a thorough medical examination to rule out any underlying mental illness.

The Catholic Church believes that an ordained priest acts on behalf of God, speaks on behalf of God, and represents the authority of God on earth. As darkness descends upon the earth, it is essential to recognize the immense revelatory awakening coming to the church of Jesus Christ. This awakening involves the realization that only a select group of priests on earth will possess the authority to speak and act on behalf of Christ, and only they will have the ability to dismantle and displace the rising tide of darkness. It is necessary to look at the past to understand the dynamics of this new company of priests.

GOD'S ORIGINAL PLAN FOR A PRIESTHOOD

Many people think that Eden was originally just a garden, but that is not entirely accurate. In the book of Genesis, Moses provides clues, indicators, and language that suggest that Eden was a temple with a garden. Eden served as a convergence point between two realms: heaven and earth. God placed Adam in Eden and gave him the mandate to be fruitful, multiply, and take dominion over the earth.

In Genesis 2:15, God gives Adam the task of "working" and "keeping" Eden. These two verbs in Hebrew are *avad* (עָבַד) and *shamar* (שָׁמַר). The Hebrew word *avad* generally means "to work" or "to serve." It is usually not used in the context of farming but rather serving in a religious context. The Hebrew word *shamar* means "to keep" or "to guard." Shamar is often used concerning the duties of priests.[1]

For example, in Exodus 28:36 (NKJV), the Lord tells Moses to make a plate of gold and engrave the words "*HOLINESS TO THE LORD.*" The plate is to be attached to the high priest's turban, "*and Aaron shall bear any guilt from the holy things that the people of Israel consecrate as their holy gifts. It shall regularly be on his forehead, that they may be accepted before the Lord"* (Exodus 28:38 ESV).

Here, the word *shamar* describes the high priest's responsibility to bear the people's guilt and ensure that the people's holy gifts are accepted before the Lord. In other words, the high priest is charged with guarding or keeping the holiness of the offerings and the people so that they remain acceptable to God.

Similarly, in Numbers 18:7 (ESV), the Lord tells Aaron:

> *You and your sons with you shall guard your priesthood for all that concerns the altar and that is within the veil, and you shall serve. I give your priesthood as a gift, and any outsider who comes near shall be put to death.*

Here, the word *shamar* is used to describe the duty of the priests to guard or keep their priesthood, which includes their responsibility for the altar and the items within the veil, the innermost part of the tabernacle. The priests are also to serve in their priestly duties and are warned that anyone coming near without authorization will be put to death.

Overall, the word *shamar* is used in the Bible to describe the duty of priests, not gardeners, to guard or keep the holiness of the things and people entrusted to their care and to ensure that they remain acceptable to God.

When used together, the words *avad* and *shamar* in Genesis 2:15 suggest that Adam was not just to tend to the plants and animals but to ensure that Eden remained a sacred and special place, a temple set apart for Yahweh and His divine counsel.

But God's original intent for humanity was not that we'd all be gardeners but rather that we would be priests who would care for and expand Eden until the entire planet became one temple for Yahweh. This plan was seriously deterred and delayed by humanity's rebellion against God. However, God showed mercy by establishing a temporary shadow city, Israel, a literal nation reflecting humanity's original calling as priests. Israel had a temple and a priesthood.

When Jesus taught His disciples how to pray, He said to ask the Father that "His kingdom would come, and that His will would be done on earth as it is in heaven." He was saying when you pray, pray that it will be again as it once was. When we get to the final book of the Bible, John's Revelation of the Christ, we see that the prayer of Jesus will be answered. In fact, at the end of the Bible, the church does not go up, but rather, heaven comes down. The New Jerusalem, the City of God, the New Eden will come down and unite with the earth, restoring all things.

Even though the fulfillment of this vision is still in the future, we do not have to wait to step back into God's original priestly call for our lives. The life, death, burial, and resurrection of Jesus Christ, our perfect High Priest and King, has initiated and ordained us into His priesthood. Therefore, we must understand our job description as priests who are called to work toward restoring God's temple on earth.

Stumbling into Priesthood

In Genesis 18:16-33, the Angel of the Lord (the embodiment of Yahweh Himself) and two angels begin their journey from Abraham's camp to the wicked city of Sodom. After God declares His intent to destroy Sodom after verifying the city's sin with the cries of injustice brought before Him, Abraham intercepts the Lord in a bold and humorous account resembling a fierce negotiation. Many speculate that since Abraham's nephew Lot and his family lived in Sodom, this was perhaps a clever intervention attempt from Abraham to get Yahweh to change his mind.

Abraham begins by asking God that if there were 50 righteous ones in the city, would He destroy the 50 righteous along with the wicked. When God says that if He finds 50, He will spare the city, Abraham then asks Him the same question, but this time inquiring of the possibility for mercy if there were 45. This dialogue continues, back and forth, between Abraham and God for quite some time until finally, Abraham gets Him down to ten people. Abraham asks, "Let's say there are only ten righteous people in the city. Will You destroy the ten righteous along with the wicked?" At this point, the Lord reveals that for the sake of the ten, He would show mercy, at which point Abraham releases the Lord to continue His journey into Sodom and returns home.

Now, what's going on here? It isn't a shrewd negotiation between Abraham and Yahweh to manipulate God to have mercy on Lot. Here is a moment of education. Abraham is inquiring of the Lord. How many righteous ones in a city does it take to make an impact? Abraham sought the Lord not just to save his nephew and family.

Abraham sought the Lord to inquire about what it would take to save a city, and in doing so, we see Abraham accidentally stumble into God's original plan for him—that he would be a priest.

I'll explain. Priests were considered to be mediators between God and the people. *Mediator* is a powerful word. It means one willing to be involved in a conflict to reach an agreement, a go-between. Priests would represent the people to the Lord, and vice versa; they would represent God to the people. Priests were to be intermediaries who acted as a link between people to bring out reconciliation. They were intercessors. Middlemen.

In this passage, Abraham, who has no authority to represent Sodom legally, steps into his priestly role and represents the people of the wicked city before the Lord. He is seeking God for His mercy on behalf of the people, and in the same way, Abraham's life would represent the will of Yahweh on the earth, pointing people to God's faithfulness and redemptive plan.

His life is the message, a sermon, a prophetic word, and an invitation to step into God's original role for humanity. The original Edenic mandate is that we would be fruitful and multiply, that we would steward the earth and transform it into the temple of Yahweh; we have been called a company of priests.

JESUS, YOUR HIGH PRIEST

As supernatural believers, it is crucial to understand and embrace the concept of Jesus as our High Priest. His sacrifice has made it possible for us to have direct access to God without needing a human mediator. We are now partakers of His divine nature, called to be ambassadors of heaven on earth.

But this is not just information to be understood intellectually; it is a charge to be lived out practically. We are called to step boldly into our identity and destiny as children of God, fully embracing our access, authority, and responsibility in both the heavens and earth. We are called to be agents of reconciliation, redemption, and advocacy for others, just as Jesus is for us.

The truth of Jesus as our High Priest should not be taken lightly or ignored. It is a call to action, to step into the fullness of who we are in Him and to walk confidently in our calling. We are called the light in the darkness, the salt of the earth, and the voice of hope to those around us.

So let us understand the concept of Jesus as our High Priest and live it out with passion and purpose. Let us boldly approach the throne of grace, knowing we have direct access to God through Jesus. Let us carry the weight of our responsibility as ambassadors of heaven, knowing that the Holy Spirit empowers us to fulfill our assignments and make a difference in the world.

ONLY A PRIESTHOOD WILL BE ABLE TO DISMANTLE THIS DARKNESS

As you end this book, I want to challenge and inspire you to take action. We live in a world full of darkness, and it's the kind of darkness that a powerful priesthood can only dismantle. As mentioned, the Catholic Church recognizes the power and authority of an ordained priest when it comes to exorcising demons. But we are learning that we, as believers, are also a part of this priesthood. Yes, you are a priest! God has chosen you to represent Him on this earth. Martin Luther said that the doctrine of the priesthood of believers is not a doctrine for theologians only, but a doctrine for every Christian. As a priest, *you* possess the power and authority of Christ. You are His hands and feet, His voice, and His representative. You can heal the sick, cleanse the lepers, raise the dead, and cast out demons. These are not just idle words; they are the reality of those who walk in the anointing of Christ.

It's your time! Time to step up and fulfill your role as a priest. You have been called to serve, give, and represent God's character, nature, and authority on the earth. Please don't waste your life trying to pull along others who are not serious about their faith. It's time for you to fully step into your supernatural nature and the fullness of your authority in Christ to bring liberty to the captives.

Remember, you are:

- A spiritual house
- A holy priesthood
- A chosen race
- A royal priesthood
- A holy nation
- A people for His own possession
- You have been given a divine mandate to bring light into the darkness, hope to the hopeless, and freedom to the captives.

So I challenge you today to join the company of priests, be equally yoked, and fulfill your role's requirements. As it is written in Matthew 10:8 (NKJV), *"Freely you have received, freely give."* May you be bold and courageous as you step out in faith and use your anointing to make a difference.

TIME FOR PRIESTLY ACTION

1. Begin to see yourself supernaturally.

Can you perceive it now? Not with your physical eyes alone, or by merely observing what everyone else sees. Can you grasp the grandeur of what God is accomplishing, what He has been working on? It is a magnificent tapestry weaving together, spanning from Genesis to Revelation. It encompasses the unity of heaven and earth, the separation and fragmentation caused by humanity's disobedience and rebellion, the establishment of the New Jerusalem, and a prophetic glimpse of what was and is yet to come. It includes the arrival of the Messiah, the reuniting of humanity with God's restorative plan, the propagation of the good news of Jesus Christ through a new priesthood, and the ultimate return of King Jesus to judge and restore all things.

Now that you understand the storyline, it's clear that your supernatural context is much more than simply participating in prophetic treasure hunts while hanging out with friends at the mall. It is about awakening a generation to their priestly purpose on earth. It's about the body of Christ taking responsibility for the gift that God has bestowed upon us. It's about realizing our authority and stepping into the chaos to bring order.

Your physical eyes will try to deceive you. They will urge you to succumb to defeat and accept the circumstances as they are. Other people's physical eyes will do the same, seeking to disqualify individuals based on their past, failures, and other disqualifying factors.

Take David, for example, who was just a young shepherd boy when he defeated the giant Goliath with a mere stone and a slingshot. Or consider Moses who, at the age of 80, led the Israelites out of Egypt. These are just a couple of examples of individuals deemed unqualified, too young, or too old, yet they accomplished great things with God's help. When you say "yes" to Jesus, He uses your weaknesses to display His strength.

Furthermore, it's also normal to get distracted by our mistakes and failures. Sometimes, we feel like we're not good enough to be used by God. However, the Bible contains examples of people who have made mistakes but still found redemption and purpose in God's plan.

Take the apostle Paul, for example. He was once a persecutor of Christians, a total hater, and vicious. Still, after encountering Jesus, he became one of the most influential figures in the early Christian church and is famous for writing "the love chapter," 1 Corinthians 13. God redeemed and used him to spread the gospel while writing a significant portion of the New Testament. Similarly, King David committed two biggies, adultery and murder, yet even after all that, he was still referred to as a man after God's own heart. When he repented of his sins, God forgave him and continued to use him as a leader of Israel.

Be encouraged! These examples remind you that no matter what you've done in the past, God's grace and forgiveness are available to you. You can find purpose and meaning in serving God, no matter how broken you feel. Shame and guilt don't have to hold you back from experiencing the fullness of God's love, grace, and power. God sees beyond all your past mistakes and weaknesses and will use even your darkest moments for His glory and your good.

As a priest, it will be essential to begin seeing the world through God's eyes. It will be imperative and critical to your calling and service to your community and the world. Viewing the world through God's eyes will provide clarity and purpose, helping you prioritize what is truly important and stay focused on your glorious and supernatural assignments. It will also deepen your relationship with the Holy Spirit, allowing you to draw on the significance of your own experiences and insights to better serve the world around you.

2. Appreciate the supernatural timing of your life here on the earth.

Appreciating the supernatural timing of our lives on earth requires a shift in perspective. Instead of focusing on the negative aspects of the world, we must see the bigger picture and understand that we have come to our royal position for such a time as this.

The prophet Isaiah reminds us of this in Isaiah 60:1 (ESV), where he says, *"Arise, shine, for your light has come, and the glory of the Lord has risen upon you."* It is a call to action to be grateful for the opportunity to serve God and be a part of His plan for humanity.

It is easy to get caught up in the negativity and darkness surrounding us, to fall into the belief and trap that this is the darkest and worst time to be alive on the earth. We must resist the temptation to grumble and complain and instead focus on the unique tools and opportunities we have now that have never been available to humanity.

Think about this: never before in the history of humanity has the world been so small and have unreached people been so reachable. Advances in transportation technology have made it easier to travel the world quickly and easily. The internet and mobile devices have transformed communication, allowing people to connect globally in real time. The global economy has become increasingly interconnected, with goods and services flowing freely across borders, creating opportunities for people to work and do business with others worldwide. The ease of travel and communication has also led to a greater appreciation and openness to new ideas. People have access to information and are searching for radical, supernatural hope—good news!

It's essential to acknowledge that some challenges and difficulties come with living in this time. It's easy to become cynical and pessimistic about the world's state and feel overwhelmed by our problems. But we must remember that with unprecedented opportunities come unprecedented responsibilities. It is up to us to use our unique tools and abilities to make a positive impact in the world and be a force for redemption unto the glory of God.

3. Don't focus on the problem; focus on the supernatural opportunity.

In the face of challenges, it can be easy to become fixated on the problem and allow it to overwhelm us. However, in the kingdom, there are no problems, only opportunities. Throughout the Bible, we find encouraging reminders that when problems arise, by God's grace, we can discover supernatural opportunities within the difficulties.

Romans 8:28 (NKJV) says, "*And we know that all things work together for good to those who love God, to those who are the called according to His purpose.*" Within every trial, if you search for them, you will find the precious ingredients needed for God to be intimately known and wondrously glorified.

Instead of allowing our problems to defeat us, we can see them as opportunities for growth and transformation. By focusing on the supernatural possibilities that lie within the darkness, we can create portals for breakthroughs and victory. These challenges can fuel our resolve against the enemy and inspire us to share our testimony of triumph with others.

So if you are facing difficulties in your life right now, don't lose heart. Instead, shift your perspective and recognize that these challenges are a chance for you to shine bright with the light of heaven and move forward toward greater things. There are supernatural kingdom opportunities within the darkness waiting for you to enter them. Don't fear the problems; fear God!

It's time to shift your perspective and see the opportunity amid the darkness. Rather than getting bogged down by problems, we must recognize that they serve as the building blocks for portals to new opportunities. These divine opportunities allow us to overcome significant obstacles, achieve major victories, and share our newfound revelation with the world.

Instead of being discouraged by life's problems, we must choose to get excited because these tribulations are the ammunition we need to fight against the enemy. Our challenges allow us to hone our skills and develop a stronger sense of resilience. They catalyze growth and progress, enabling us to shine light in the darkness.

So shift your focus away from the problem and instead embrace the possibilities that await you on the other side. With a prophetic perspective and a determination to overcome, you can (and will) partner with Holy Spirit to flip tribulations into triumphs and become a beacon of hope for those around you.

4. Give God your "yes!"

The call to give God our "yes" is not new. Throughout the Bible, we see individuals who answered God's call with a resounding affirmation, and it changed their lives forever. In Genesis 12:1-3, God called Abram to leave his country and family and go to a land He would show him. Abram responded with a "yes" and became the father of many nations.

Similarly, in the New Testament the disciples dropped everything and followed Jesus when He called them. They gave Him their "yes," and it transformed their lives and the course of history. In Luke 5:8 (ESV), after Jesus performs a miracle and fills their boats with fish, Simon Peter falls at His feet and says, *"Depart from me, for I am a sinful man, O Lord."* Yet, when Jesus tells him, *"Do not be afraid; from now on, you will be catching men*" (Luke 5:10 ESV), Simon Peter and his partners James and John leave everything and follow Jesus.

Giving God our "yes" means surrendering our will and desires to Him, trusting Him with our lives and future. It means putting aside our fears and doubts and stepping out in faith, knowing He will never leave or forsake us. As we give God our "yes," He will equip us with His nature and power, and His flashes of lightning and wonders will flow through us with a new intensity, accuracy, and momentum.

So let us not merely wait for God or be open to Him, but let us give Him our "yes" with all our hearts and minds, just as the psalmist says in Psalm 119:10 (ESV), "*With my whole heart I seek you; let me not wander from your commandments.*" Let us choose to follow Jesus, live for Him, be ministers of His nature and power, and watch as He transforms our lives and the lives of those around us.

5. Advance.

My friends, it is time to embrace the call to expand Eden. Just as God commanded Adam and Eve to cultivate and keep the garden of Eden, we, too, are called to cultivate and expand the kingdom of God here on earth. American theologian and professor Richard Mouw addressed the tension that exists between being a priest on the earth and the call to advance; he said, "The priesthood of believers is not a license for individualism or isolationism, but a call to community and cooperation in the mission of Christ."

This advancement requires us to appreciate growth, which demands change. As it is written in Ecclesiastes 3:1 (NKJV),

"To everything there is a season, a time for every purpose under heaven." We must be willing to let go of what used to be and embrace the new things that the Lord is about to birth through us.

This advancement means transition and promotion! Just as God promoted Joseph from a prisoner to a ruler in Egypt, He is also willing to promote us as we faithfully obey Him. However, we must remember that obedience is critical. In Deuteronomy 28:1, God promises blessings for those who obey His commands. Therefore, we must honor God in this desire to advance and strive to be led by obedience unto the Lord lest our self-ambition become our ultimate motivator, craving power for ourselves. God's will is accomplished through our obedience.

As it is written in Micah 6:8 (NKJV), *"He has shown you, O man, what is good; and what does the Lord require of you but to do justly, to love mercy, and to walk humbly with your God?"* Let us humble ourselves before the Lord and seek to do His will.

In conclusion, comparing our kingdom's advancements to others is a dangerous trap that can lead us down the wrong path. It can make us feel inadequate or cause us to become prideful, both of which are not in line with God's will. Success in the kingdom of God is not measured by earthly standards such as wealth, status, or power. Instead, it is measured by our obedience to God's commands and willingness to serve Him.

As followers of Christ, we must shift our focus from earthly treasures to treasures in heaven. The treasures we lay up in heaven are not subject to the same decay and destruction as earthly treasures. They are eternal and cannot be taken away from us. We can lay up treasures in heaven by faithfully obeying God and serving Him with our hearts.

Therefore, let us not fall into the trap of comparing ourselves to others or seeking earthly recognition and success. Instead, let us seek to lay up treasures in heaven through faithful obedience to God. Let us focus on serving Him with all we have and trust that He will reward us with treasures that will last for eternity. May we be faithful stewards of God's gifts and always seek to glorify Him in everything we do.

ACTIVATION PRAYER

Dear heavenly Father,

Thank You for the precious gift of Your son, Jesus Christ, who makes it possible for us to be partakers of Your divine nature and to live this unapologetically supernatural life. We pray that You will help us to see ourselves supernaturally and to grasp the grandeur of what You are accomplishing in our world.

We should be reminded that even when we are weak, we use our weaknesses to display our strengths. Help us not to be distracted by our mistakes and failures but to remember that You redeem and use even our darkest moments for Your glory and our good.

Father, we also ask that You help us appreciate the supernatural timing of our lives here on earth. Please give us a shift in perspective so we may see the bigger picture and understand that we are here for such a time. May we resist the temptation to grumble and complain but instead focus on the unique tools and opportunities we have now, which have never been available to humanity.

May we view the world through Your eyes, gain clarity and purpose, and stay focused on our glorious and supernatural assignments. May we also deepen our relationship with the Holy Spirit, allowing us to draw on the significance of our own experiences and insights to better serve the world around us.

Thank You for the privilege of being part of Your plan for humanity. Please help us to take responsibility for the gift You have bestowed upon us and to use it to bring about order in a chaotic world. We ask all these things in the name of Jesus Christ, our Lord and Savior.

Amen.

NOTE

1. Forerunner Commentary, qtd. in Bible Study Tools, "What the Bible says about Shamar," accessed May 7, 2023, https://www.bibletools.org/index.cfm/fuseaction/topical.show/RTD/cgg/ID/2169/Shamar.htm.

ABOUT DARREN STOTT

Darren Stott is a supernaturalist called by God to catalyze joy through anointed media, books, entertainment, and equipping resources. He is the founder of Supernaturalist Ministry, and he serves as the CEO of Renaissance Coalition, a movement incorporated by John G. Lake's daughter in Spokane, Washington, in 1947. He is the Senior Leader of Seattle Revival Center.

In the Right Hands, This Book Will Change Lives!

Most of the people who need this message will not be looking for this book. To change their lives, you need to **put a copy of this book in their hands.**

Our ministry is constantly seeking methods to find the people who need this anointed message to change their lives. **Will you help us reach these people?**

Extend this ministry by sowing three, five, ten, or *even more* books today and change people's lives for the better! Your generosity will be part of catalyzing the Great Awakening that many have been prophesying and praying for.

Check out
our **Destiny Image**
bestsellers page at
destinyimage.com/bestsellers

for cutting-edge,
prophetic messages
that will supernaturally
empower you and the
body of Christ.

From
Troy A. Brewer

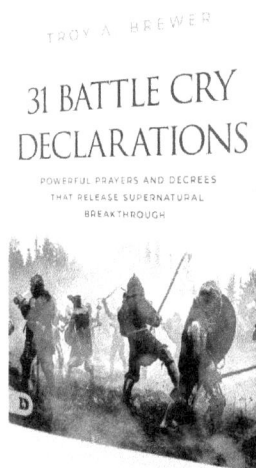

TROY A. BREWER

31 BATTLE CRY DECLARATIONS

POWERFUL PRAYERS AND DECREES
THAT RELEASE SUPERNATURAL
BREAKTHROUGH

YOUR SPIRITUAL ARSENAL AWAITS WITHIN.
ARE YOU READY TO CLAIM IT?

When battles rage against the forces of darkness, you need more than mere faith—you need weapons. Weapons forged in holy fire, to pierce the heart of darkness and dispel the oppressive forces that seek to stifle your soul.

Troy Brewer, renowned pastor, minister, and prophet, hands you the very tools of the trade. With 31 potent and practical declarations, he equips you to not just stand your ground, but reclaim it. Every word, every decree, rooted deeply in the victory of the cross, serves as both shield and sword against the onslaught of demonic assignments.

Troy's challenge to you is clear: Don't just witness the power of the cross. Wield it. Become a conqueror, reverse the tide from loss to victory, and emerge not just a believer, but a spiritual conqueror.

Purchase your copy wherever books are sold

From

JerriAnn Webb

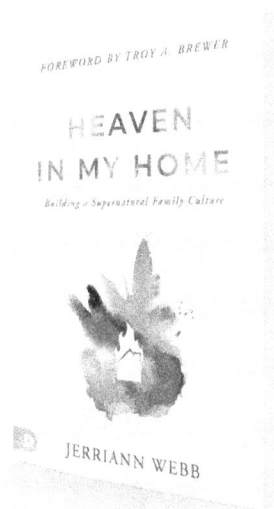

Experience the Power and Peace of Heaven in Your Home!

Through today's culture, the enemy has declared war on your family. Relentless attacks from television, movies, and social media chip away at your hope for change. You long for a home marked by encounter and presence, but most days are marked by weariness and resignation.

Yet change—even transformation—is possible under your roof.

In *Heaven in My Home*, spiritual leader and family expert JerriAnn Webb empowers you to overcome the discouragement and dysfunction in your home to become a healthy, Holy Spirit-filled family that will change the world.

Don't settle for society's status quo or strife-filled days. Fight back by creating a culture marked by the Father's supernatural hope, healing, transformation, and power. Revival for your family starts with you, flowing from your heart into your home—and then to the world.

Purchase your copy wherever books are sold

www.ingramcontent.com/pod-product-compliance
Lightning Source LLC
Chambersburg PA
CBHW070840100426

42813CB00003B/686